CRIME AND PUNISHMENT
in
VICTORIAN LONDON

For Harris, Gilly and Bagel

CRIME AND PUNISHMENT
in
VICTORIAN LONDON

*A Street-level View of the
City's Underworld*

Ross Gilfillan

findmypast.co.uk
search with the experts

PEN & SWORD
HISTORY

First published in Great Britain in 2014 by
PEN AND SWORD HISTORY
an imprint of
Pen and Sword Books Ltd
47 Church Street
Barnsley
South Yorkshire S70 2AS

ISBN 978 1 78159 342 4

Printed and bound in England
by CPI Group (UK) Ltd, Croydon, CR0 4YY

Typeset in Times New Roman by
CHIC GRAPHICS

Pen & Sword Books Ltd incorporates the imprints of
Pen & Sword Books Ltd incorporates the imprints of Pen & Sword
Archaeology, Atlas, Aviation, Battleground, Discovery, Family
History, History, Maritime, Military, Naval, Politics, Railways, Select,
Social History, Transport, True Crime, and Claymore Press, Frontline
Books, Leo Cooper, Praetorian Press, Remember When, Seaforth
Publishing and Wharncliffe..

For a complete list of Pen and Sword titles please contact
Pen and Sword Books Limited
47 Church Street, Barnsley, South Yorkshire, S70 2AS, England
E-mail: enquiries@pen-and-sword.co.uk
Website: www.pen-and-sword.co.uk

Contents

Introduction

The dark side of Victorian life continues to grip the popular imagination. Turn on the television, go to the movies, or browse in a bookshop and you'll be sure to encounter some work of the imagination or of diligent research, which summons up once again the ramshackle doss-houses and brothels of the East End, the festering stink of the slums and the blood-stained streets of fog-bound, murderous Whitechapel. Heartless confidence tricks, vicious assaults and villainous homicides are still being re-enacted more than a century after they were committed. It's as though under the modern map of London still lies the palimpsest of an older, apparently more dangerous city, which has never quite gone away.

Authors have fed on this peculiar fascination for the underbelly of Victorian life since the days when the world they described was still fresh in the mind. Charles Dickens knew the value of bringing the seamier side of London on to his pages. Dickens populated his novels with the poor, the hungry and the criminal characters that better-heeled London preferred not to see – unless safely served up in serialised fiction, or in the newspaper columns of journalist Henry Mayhew's long-running exposé of life on the streets of mid-century London. Dickens shocked readers with stories of callous fiends preying on homeless children, tragic suicides fished from the Thames and the brutal murder of Nancy by the thuggish burglar Bill Sykes. Drawing on his own experiences of visiting hellish places like Jacob's Island in Bermondsey, Dickens gave middle-class readers a glimpse of life on the other side of the recently-laid tracks. Just as Mayhew did, he gave voices to people on the streets, from pickpockets like the Artful Dodger to trouble-beset innocents like Little Dorrit, and even to Jo, a lowly crossing sweeper.

But Dickens wasn't writing only to draw attention to social evils.

INTRODUCTION

He readily perceived that with his unorthodox characters drawn from this unseen side of London life, he had tapped into a suppressed and sometimes ghoulish appetite. It was an appetite that he and others like him were ready to satisfy. Other possibilities also offered themselves. With Sergeant Rose and Inspector Bucket, Dickens and his friend Wilkie Collins introduced the first detectives into fiction. Dickens and Collins, and later, Conan Doyle, were among a body of writers who realised that the work of the new detective force could add narrative drive to their fiction. They gave birth to a genre whose popularity shows no sign of diminishing, and is one reason why the world they described remains such a fertile ground for writers, too.

Recent years have seen authors drawing on the legacy of their Victorian forebears and finding a ready readership for stories set in an age that is alien in many respects but which, with its insistent drive towards modernity, is still recognisable as the foundations of our own. Popular books which have faithfully recreated the era include the best-selling *The Suspicions of Mr Whicher*, and the suitably Victorian-length novels, *The Quincunx* and *The Crimson Petal and the White*. Screen writers frequently revisit this milieu: Sherlock Holmes has had both TV and film updates, Dr Who regularly slips back to nineteenth century London, while the murders attributed to Jack the Ripper will always, it seems, provide fodder for fiction.

The period we cover has its main focus on the the middle years of the nineteenth century, the 1850s and 1860s. Yet it also reaches back to the beginning of that century – when the murders on the Ratcliff Highway shocked London and woke minds to the idea that something must be done to improve the *ad hoc* policing of the capital – and to the century's last years, when the Ripper stalked the streets of Whitechapel.

Between these ghastly events are 60 or 70 years during which many of the factors making London a lively, often dangerous place changed dramatically. Roads were driven through thieves' rookeries, Forster's Education Act provided elementary education for all children between the ages of five and twelve, and the justice system was radically overhauled. By mid-century, the 200 capital crimes on the books in 1800 had been reduced to a mere handful. Criminals no longer upped their game on the grounds that they 'might as well be hung for a sheep as a lamb' and juries were less likely to let off a man to avoid seeing him hang. Capital punishment continued to be applied, but executions (after 1868) no longer made grisly spectacles and provided free entertainment outside the walls of Newgate.

Attitudes to crime and punishment see-sawed: flogging for instance, was on the way out before the garrotting panic of 1862 caused an increase in its application. There were even voices speaking out against capital punishment *per se*. Prison sentences replaced hanging and transportation as the most common punishments, new prisons were built, and well-meaning experiments with solitary confinement were made.

A succession of seismic changes were wrought in this age, not only in social conditions but also in the city itself. Some of the neighbourhoods which bred the crime that made the city dangerous – or were perceived as such by an expanding, increasingly sensation-hungry press – were wiped from the map. Government bodies, philanthropic individuals, religious and other charitable institutions gradually brought about their own improvements to the common lot. However, there was still widespread poverty and concomitant social evils by the century's end. This often turbulent century had coped, or tried to cope, with social unrest and hunger caused by the introduction of machinery into industry, the Corn Laws, (which made the buying of cheap foreign grain prohibitively expensive), and the new Poor Laws (which allowed relief for the poverty-stricken only through the harsh workhouse system). The towns and cities had an influx of agricultural workers untrained for urban industrial occupations and refugees from the famine in Ireland. No wonder there had been an explosion of crime on the streets.

Taking the century as a whole, though, it was probably safer to live in London during the nineteenth century than it had been in centuries past. It might not have seemed so, of course, now that crime was accounted for in figures and its details rapidly and widely disseminated, but by the century's end, there was an operational police force, which didn't just deter but now also tried to solve crimes, and a more humane approach to punishment. Despite this, preceding centuries have signally failed to fascinate succeeding generations in the same way the nineteenth century so evidently has.

One reason for this is because this century has left much more of an imprint. In the newspaper archives, in surviving photographs and in public records are the first-hand accounts, the documented histories and sometimes the faces of people who got through their hard lives as best they could. There are records too, of what happened to them when it all went awry and they faced the 'full majesty of the law'. The crimes and calamitous mistakes of this century, originally reported in newspapers and broadsides, or only gleaned from ballads and melodramatic renditions in theatres, have been passed down almost as folkloric stories, entering the oral tradition and then being rediscovered and reused by successions of writers for their own purposes.

Within this book you'll meet – and often hear from in their own words – some of the people whose circumstances and actions gave birth to the stories and legends that make this dark side of London's history memorable for all the wrong reasons. Perhaps the best and certainly the most exhaustive accounts of people like these come from Henry Mayhew, whose extraordinarily detailed writings, and illuminating interviews with London's poor and dispossessed, were collected and published in four volumes as *London Labour and the London Poor* in 1851.

So it is with Henry Mayhew that we must begin...

On a warm September evening in 1852, the journalist Henry Mayhew prepares to ascend from London's Vauxhall Pleasure Gardens in a hot air balloon. These flights are still novel enough to get star billing on advertising posters and a small crowd has gathered to witness the spectacle. Faces in the basket glow, ruddy in the fiery light from burners inflating the great balloon, which strains against taut ropes. When the last stragglers have joined the spectators and it seems that the balloon might tear itself from the earth at any moment, a gun is fired and the ropes are loosed.

And Henry sees the ground plunge suddenly away. Peering over the rim of the basket, he observes flat, upturned faces and fluttering hands getting smaller as the humming of conversations and the excited cries of children grow faint. Higher he rises, leaving the pleasure gardens with their lantern-lit walkways and desultory strollers far below. The music from the orchestra fades as the great gas bag climbs through London's smoky atmosphere and catches the gentlest of breezes, which starts to carry it in the direction of Richmond. Henry is surprised to feel no sensation of movement. The experience is rather, he'll say, like that of seeing a series of fascinating scenes being pulled smoothly beneath him by invisible hands.

And what fascinating scenes they are. Either side of the perniciously odorous, serpentine Thames – so choked with shipping that you almost might cross it without wetting your feet – are countless thousands of buildings, a smoke-blackened *bricken mass* from whose chimney pots rises the dense breath of a million coal fires – which, thankfully, Henry is finally rising above. From this elevation, the city looks like a mostly dun-coloured, but infinitely more detailed, version of Cross's new map of London. Henry is amazed at the reduction in scale; great locomotives puff steam like domestic kettles, enormous brewers' drays and horse-drawn buses on gas-lit streets are only children's toys, while the people walking in the bright West End might be bugs on a glass. Henry is enthralled, *gobsmacked*, if you like, by his new perspective on 'churches and hospitals, banks and prisons, palaces and workhouses'. He notes too, the 'docks and refuges for the destitute, parks and squares and courts and alleys'.

Henry examines it all as an entomologist might examine a beetle. Because Henry too is a scientist of sorts, though the social sciences are so new that he has yet to be recognised as a pioneer of social research. Henry's field of study has been London itself, in particular its workers and those who can not, or *will not*, work and who subsist through a variety of interesting other means. Undoubtedly, Henry Mayhew knows more about the 'average man in the street' than any one of the distant mites he sees streaming across the river and funnelling into Waterloo Bridge Station.

Ever since 1849, when he wrote to the *Morning Chronicle* about the lethally insanitary conditions endured by residents of Bermondsey, Henry has been contributing an extraordinary series of daily articles to this newspaper. Serious in intent, yet often sensational in content, these have become compulsive reading for many whose eyes Henry is opening to a side of London they have never seen, or perhaps have consciously ignored. Henry has, in his obsessive and painstaking way, been amassing enormous amounts of data about working-class life in London and purveying it for *Chronicle* readers in digestible form. Comfortable London has been shocked, appalled and perhaps secretly excited to discover a fantastic, implausible and sometimes highly dangerous world existing just beyond its doorstep.

Shadowy faces passed in the street – the crossing sweepers, cress-sellers, chimney sweeps and flower-girls, the street showmen, the rat-catchers, the 'pure' finders (who collect dogs' excrement for use by tanners) and even the beggars – now have voices and histories, because Mayhew has drawn out their stories and has retailed them, as closely as possible, in their own words. Mayhew has introduced his readers to people whom extreme poverty has reduced to unimaginable occupations: the toshers, who crawl through sewers in search of dropped coins and the bare-footed mudlarks, children who risk septicaemia and disease on the muddy banks of the Thames in their search for bits of iron, lengths of old rope, lumps of coal or anything else which might turn a penny.

He has ventured deep into territory unknown and very often feared by his readers, though this alien land is very often only a few streets distant. He's gone among the sailors and their prostitutes on the ramshackle Ratcliffe Highway and, in the protective company of police officers, has infiltrated the low lodging houses and thieves' dens of Spitalfields and Whitechapel. In the course of his investigations, Mayhew has encountered any number of thieves, swindlers, prostitutes and those for whom ends will always justify means. These experiences have led him to conclude that there is in London 'more iniquity, more wealth and more want ... than in any other part of the earth'.

Crime looms large in the minds of Londoners, especially those with property to protect. All over the city, watches, purses and handkerchiefs have been disappearing from pockets, goods are migrating from warehouses, off docks and out of shop windows. Burglaries are rife, shoplifting is carried on in West End stores and people fall victim to all kinds of frauds and ingenious swindles. Pornographers proliferate – most notably in Holywell Street – and an estimated 80,000 prostitutes are operating, a great many quite openly, on the streets of the capital. The vulnerable are robbed in dark alleys and a new kind of mugging called garrotting, in which the victim is half-strangled from behind while being stripped of his possessions, is fascinating the editors of newspapers. No wonder people are turning to the *Chronicle* to find out more.

The causes of this epidemic of crime will perhaps become apparent if we leave Henry to float serenely towards Richmond and make our way into some of the capital's less salubrious districts, where we'll meet some of those interesting characters responsible for London's soaring crime figures.

CRIME

CHAPTER 1

'You've Got to Pick A Pocket or Two'
Embarking on a life of crime

Dick is a sad-looking man with a sallow complexion, whose beard and moustache age him beyond his 31 years. He's already had a long life of picking pockets, and regular spells in prison – where he spent months in solitary confinement – have taken a heavy toll. His story is typical of many, but when Henry Mayhew (or his colleague, John Binny) interviews him at a low lodging house in 1861, this hopeless recidivist proves to be a well-read and intelligent man.

Mayhew believes that pickpockets are generally the products of neglectful or drunken parents, or parents who themselves are already thieves, but the man Mayhew calls 'Dick' bucks the trend – he has been brought up in a strict Wesleyan household near Shrewsbury. His father, a minister, forbade him to stay out late and held services of worship every evening. Despite being his father's favourite, the wilful Dick rebelled and, before he was ten years old, he took the four sovereigns of pocket money he had saved and boarded a coach bound for London. There are more than a few parallels with *Oliver Twist* in what happens next.

"When I got to London I had neither friend nor acquaintance," he says. "I first put up at a coffee shop in the Mile End Road and lodged there for seven weeks, until my money was nearly all spent." His next address was a "mean lodging house" in Field Lane, Holborn, where he "met with characters I had never seen before and heard language I had not formerly heard". He stopped there for almost three weeks, doing nothing but no doubt learning a lot, until his money ran out. The landlady allowed him to stay on for a few more days, after which he was turned out of doors, perfectly ignorant, he admits, in the ways and means of getting a living in London.

There's a horrible inevitability about what happens next. "I was taken by several poor ragged boys to sleep in the dark arches of the Adelphi", he recalls. Here, he "often saw boys follow the male passengers when the boats came to the Adelphi stairs". When the passengers had finished disembarking from the boats, Dick finds that his companions generally have "one or two handkerchiefs". The boys then introduce the young Dick to a shifty man called 'Larry', a meeting which takes place in the unusual location of a (presumably abandoned) prison van. Larry, as he discovers, gives the boys whatever price he likes for the handkerchiefs. If they don't agree, he threatens to have them arrested.

Dick's own initiation into the pickpocketing line is not long in coming. "The boys had been very kind, sharing what they got with me, but always asking why I did not try my hand", he says. "I was ashamed to live any longer upon the food they gave me without doing something for myself". There is, of course, someone on hand to help with his transition from penniless waif to budding criminal. His name is Joe and Joe is there to see that Dick goes through with his first pocket-picking. One evening, by the banks of the river, they see "an elderly gentleman step ashore and a lady with him. They had," he adds, "a little dog, with a string attached to it, that they led along".

Joe 'fans', or lightly feels the pocket of their victim, and then tells Dick to try his luck. "I went close to the gentleman's side", Dick says, "trembling all the time". He remembers Joe standing nearby in the dark. Dick goes with his intended victim "up the steep hill of the Adelphi...Joe still following us, encouraging me all the time, while the old gentleman was engaged with the little dog". Then Dick makes his move, dipping his hand into the pocket and retrieving its contents, apparently without the victim's notice. "I took out a green 'kingsman'", he says, explaining that this is "next in value to a black silk handkerchief". Immediately after the theft, they "went to the arches, where Larry was, and Joe said to him, 'there is Dick's first trial...you

4

must give him a ray [*1s 6d*] for it.' After a deal of pressing, we got one shilling".

The successful result and easy money fill Dick with confidence. In fact, he appears to have discovered a natural talent. "In the course of a few weeks, I was considered the cleverest of the little band, never failing to get a couple of handkerchiefs from passengers of each docking boat". His skills don't go unnoticed: he's befriended by contacts of Larry, two young and well-dressed men, who give the boy presents and encourage his activities. Then, after being caught red-handed, he is sentenced to two months in Westminster Bridewell. On his release, the young men have a cab waiting to drive him to their own home, where Dick will now live.

Under their tutelage, Dick becomes adept at robbing purses from ladies. To do this he must play the part of a gentleman's son, and to this end, he is newly clothed in a little surtout-coat, trousers and a beaver hat. The outfit is completed by a black silk necktie and collar. Practising on Emily, one of the men's girlfriends, Dick becomes proficient at stealing ladies' purses and the men are soon benefitting from their charge's skills. The booty is divided equally and one day, Dick finds he has netted himself £19, which he blows on a silver watch, a gold chain and an overcoat to carry over his left arm to cover his movements. He is unrecognisable as the starving urchin befriended by the boys of the Adelphi arches.

But it's not long before he's again apprehended and this time, he's sentenced to three months in Bridge Street Bridewell at Blackfriars, during which time he is supplied with meat and pastries, sent in by his attentive new friends. Returning to his life of crime, Dick finds that theatres are a highly promising venue for his skills. "I have often had as many as six or seven ladies' purses in the rear of the boxes", he tells Mayhew, tipping him that it's "easier to pick a female's pocket when she has several children with her to attract her attention". Crowded places have always attracted pickpockets, and in Victorian London, they operate successfully at busy railway stations, on riverboats and at any large events where their actions stand a fair chance of being obscured by the confusion of the crowd. Dick 'dips' in the well-attended

Madame Tussauds and then at the Epsom races – where, trying against his better judgement to rob "two ladies as they were stepping into a carriage" after the Derby, he is apprehended and detained once again.

After four more months, he is released. Dick's now 13 years old and this is when, he says, "I first kept a woman….She was a tall, thin, genteel girl about 15 years of age". In the cramped and foetid world of the low lodging houses, it wasn't unusual to find adolescents living together as man and wife. The sleeping arrangements for many residents appalled commentators of the time. Dick is honest enough to admit that he "often ill-used and beat her". At this point he has seen only the Bridewells, or places of short-stay detention. His first real stretch of imprisonment is spent in Tothill Fields Prison, which is then operating a rigid silent system. For Dick, being forbidden to communicate with his fellow prisoners comes as an awful shock: "The silent system was very strict", he says, "and being very wilful, I was often under punishment. It had such an effect on me that for the last six weeks of my imprisonment, I was in the infirmary".

But neither this, nor a further stretch in Coldbath Fields, changes his ways and in April 1848, Dick is to be found among the Chartists on Kennington Common, where he takes "several ladies' purses, amounting to £3 or £4" and then a gentleman's pocketbook in which, amazingly, is a bundle of bank notes amounting to £135, a small fortune at the time. And his luck holds, or so he says. "The same afternoon I took a purse in Trafalgar Square with eighteen sovereigns in it". The amounts are scarcely credible and it's only because Mayhew (or his colleague John Binny) accepts this without question that we will have to give him the benefit of the doubt.

Dick joins the greatest crowds of 1851, preying on visitors to the Great Exhibition, but perhaps doesn't do as well as he expects, because soon after this he is persuaded to join a team of cracksmen, or burglars. After a successful debut in which their booty, "silks, handkerchiefs and other drapery goods" are carried away by cab and quickly disposed of to a fence, they try a third burglary in the City, at a shop selling Geneva watches. Unfortunately, the proprietor has stayed late to do his accounts and is still on the premises at one am, when the break-in is made.

"On seeing us, he made an outcry and struggled with us", Dick says. "Assistance came immediately. Two policemen ran up to the house…We tried to make for the door…I got away and fled, when I was stunned by a man who carried a closed umbrella. Hearing the cry of 'Stop, thief!' he drew out the umbrella and I fell as I was running". This earns him 18 months in Holloway (not then a women's prison) where solitary confinement again has a deleterious effect on his health.

Finally, Dick had had enough of a life which brought him as much stress and trouble as occasional riches and the prodigal returned home to Shrewsbury. We don't know how he accounted for his time in London, nor anything of the suspicions his family must have had. But it was not long before this city thief tired of the country and returned to his old life in London. After a final stint in Coldbath Fields – and a warning that another court appearance would mean certain transportation – Dick gave up pickpocketing and at the time when Mayhew elicits his story, has settled for the life of a street patterer. Or so he claims.

Victorian Gang Violence:
the Elephant and Castle Boys and the Green Gate Gang

There's nothing new about gang culture. The nineteenth century saw teenaged street gangs battling in London and in many of the country's major conurbations. While the London gangs from the densely populated East End are particularly feared because they are apt to carry guns, gangs from Birmingham, Liverpool and Manchester cause more mayhem.

Manchester's street fighters are known as 'Scuttlers' and on one occasion, as many as 500 took part in a vicious clash over territory. Their weapons of choice are sticks, stones, knives and leather belts, which are wrapped tightly around their fists so that the heavy brass buckle makes an effective knuckleduster. Manchester's gangs are easily identifiable by their uniform dress. Scuttlers wear pointed, brass-tipped clogs, bell-bottomed trousers and silk scarves. Their haircuts are distinctive too: short back and sides, with long 'donkey' fringes worn over the left eye. Peaked caps complete the look.

Gangs are named after their local streets and areas. If London has the Elephant and Castle Boys, the Green Gate gang from Hoxton and the Dove Row gang from Hackney, then Manchester has its Bengal Tigers (from Bengal Street) and Holland Street gangs. The Scuttlers are first recorded clashing in the streets in the 1870s, but this particular spate of gang street-fighting persists into the late 1890s.

Skirmishes with other gangs offer slum kids a taste of excitement, the chance to earn respect from their peers and to retain a sense of identity in overcrowded, industrial streets. Violence also offers them a fast track to Strangeways prison. In a heavy-handed reaction to what the modern media now likes to call 'the rising tide of violence', lengthy sentences are imposed, and some Scuttlers face the lash.

Andrew Davies, Senior Lecturer in History at the University of Liverpool, has made a study of Manchester's Victorian street gangs and notes that a very great many Scuttlers were jailed. 'In the first 12 months of the so-called Rochdale Road War of 1870-71, around 500 Scuttlers were convicted and members of the local council were growing quite alarmed at the sheer number of 12 and 13-year-old boys who were languishing in prison. So, the resort to imprisonment was made very early, with sentences being handed out of 15–20 years. And somewhat to the astonishment of the authorities, this wasn't enough to stamp the practice out'.

Interviewed by a *Guardian* journalist in 1898, four Ancoats gang members say they only feel safe on their own patch and only go into the city in groups to assure safety. The reporter asks how fights get started and receives the telling reply, "You just soap your hair over your left eye and put on a pigeon-board cap. Then you walk into Salford".

Dick's lodging house is much like the 200 others Mayhew counts in this and other low-rent areas. Homes for labourers, costermongers, pedlars and anyone else who can afford nothing better, some are actually quite clean and respectable places. The lower ground floor is often the common room, in which there may be deal tables and forms to sit on. A constantly burning fire provides somewhere for the residents to cook their meals – typically a bit of fish to go with potatoes, bread and a jug of tea – and a place to dry wet clothes.

The necessaries for an evening meal can sometimes be bought on the premises, while rooms and even beds might be shared. Mayhew visits lodging houses in some of the roughest areas and is surprised, at one such location, to find a man making delicate artificial flowers at one table and at another, someone quietly reading. This isn't the scene at some of the more lively lodging houses he inspects in the protective company of a police officer.

The phrase 'breeding places for crime' perfectly describes the conditions in some low lodging houses, whose rooms are already filled with felons of one kind or another. It is as if, Mayhew says, there has been a tacit agreement as to which class of person the house will accept. As well as houses used by street sellers and other traders, there are establishments – 'flash houses' – inhabited almost exclusively by thieves and prostitutes. In the lodging house in which a "trustworthy man" is obliged to stay, "all was dilapidation, filth and noisomness". In the morning, Mayhew says, he filled a basin from a bucket in order to wash. "In the water", Mayhew says, "were floating alive, bugs and lice, which my informant was convinced had fallen from the ceiling, shaken off by the tread of someone walking in the rickety apartments above".

From the outside, many of these places look much like ordinary houses, we are told, though they may well be dirtier. The grimy windows, as one resident tells Mayhew, "are not to let the light in, but to keep the cold out". The proprietors of these houses have been able to launch their ventures on a shoestring, buying up furniture no one else will take – sometimes because it comes from houses in which cholera has taken hold – and using every inch of space. The more successful landlords "may be classed as capitalists", Mayhew says. "One…has a country house in Hampstead". The landlords will often employ deputies to oversee the running of their properties. This is not a function always, or even often, performed properly.

"Some of the lodging-houses", Mayhew claims, "are of the worst class of low brothels, and some may even be described as brothels for children". Mayhew is clearly shocked by "the licentiousness" he uncovers: "Men and women, boys and girls…herd together promiscuously". Boys, he claims, "boastfully carried on loud conversations…of their triumphs over the virtue of girls, and girls have laughed at, and encouraged the recital". Some lodging houses are fronts for fences, traders in stolen property, and the food cooked in the kitchens is often thieved from local markets by light-fingered lodgers.

The shock of finding oneself in such a place can be greater for those who have known something better. A man who "had filled a commercial situation of no little importance" but ruined himself through drink, left a rather pathetic description of the place to which his intemperance led him:

> *I myself have slept in the top room of a house not far from Drury Lane, and you could study the stars, if you were so minded, through the holes left by the slates having blown off the roof. It was a fine summer's night and the openings in the roof were then rather an advantage, for they admitted air and the room wasn't so foul as it might have been without them. I never went there again, but you may judge what thoughts went through a man's mind – a man who had seen prosperous days – as he lay in a place like that, without being able to sleep, watching the sky.*

There were times when the same man slept in rooms so overcrowded – sometimes 30 sleepers were shoe-horned into a space meant for 12 – when the atmosphere was unbearably noxious. "Their breaths in the dead of night…in the unventilated chamber", he says, "rose in one foul, choking steam of stench". It was even worse when popular events such as Greenwich Fair or the Epsom races were held and itinerant hawkers added to the problem of overcrowding: "It was not only that two or even three persons jammed themselves into a bed not too large for one full-sized man, but between the beds…were placed shakes-down, or temporary accommodation for nightly slumber. In the better lodging houses, the shakes-down are small palliasses or mattresses; in the worst, they are bundles of rags of any kind. Loose straw is only used in the country".

At busy times, people sleep on the floor, or huddle in the kitchens. The prospect of ending up in such places could fill people with "fear or horror", Mayhew says, and he allows one of his subjects to mention an instance of unusual behaviour on the part of some "decent mechanics" who have been newly-ruined. "I have reason to believe", the subject tells Mayhew, "that a person, once well-off, who has sunk into the very depths of poverty, often makes his first appearance in one of those places. Perhaps it is because he keeps away from them as long as he can, and then, in a sort of desperation [*sic*] fit, goes into the cheapest he meets with". The man explains the thinking behind this as, "I may as well know the worst at once".

Another unfortunate puts it this way: "When a man's lost caste in society, he may as well go the whole hog, bristles and all, and a low lodging-house is the entire pig".

While slum clearances have begun, London still contains pockets of awfulness. One of the foulest places to live is Jacob's Island, in Bermondsey, which is where Dickens locates Fagin's den. When Henry Mayhew writes to the *Morning Chronicle* about this place, he describes living conditions unimaginable today: 'a foul, stagnant ditch…makes an island of this pestilential spot', he says. This 'capital of cholera' as he calls it, (the epidemic of the same year is just beginning to wind down) 'has the smell of the graveyard'. He adds that 'as soon as you cross one of the crazy and rotting bridges over the reeking ditch…you know as surely as if you had chemically tested it… that the air is thickly charged with deadly gas'.

Mayhew describes open privies hanging over the water and 'dark streaks of filth' on the walls where 'the drains of each house discharge themselves into the ditch' and is horrified to be assured this is the only water the wretched inhabitants have to drink. When Mayhew ventures onto the island in 1849, it is still easily recognisable from Charles Dickens's description of it in *Oliver Twist*, which was published in 1838: 'In Jacob's Island', Dickens's narrator says, 'The warehouses are roofless and empty; the walls are crumbling down; the windows are windows no more; the doors are falling into the streets, the chimneys are blackened, but they yield no smoke'. These houses have no owners, he says, but 'are broken open and entered upon by those who...must have powerful motives for a secret residence, or be reduced to a destitute condition indeed'. A perfect horror of a place but an ideal setting for the lair of Fagin and his ragged gang of pickpockets.

But Bermondsey is far from being the only district written off as a thieves' rookery, though it may well be the least sanitary. Out-and-out thieves' dens, the homes to pickpockets, cadgers, sneak thieves and prostitutes, are still common in areas such as Spitalfields, Whitechapel and Seven Dials – and its contiguous neighbouring parish, the notorious St Giles.

The first thing to say about St Giles-in-the-Fields is that it's no longer 'in the fields'. By the mid-nineteenth century, there is only the vaguest memory of a formerly pleasant semi-rural village within a hour's walk of the City of London. The fields have long gone. Various factors have led to this hamlet becoming a vastly overcrowded and unhealthy slum, many of them linked with disasters of one kind or another. St Giles has a history of mopping up the fallout of trouble elsewhere. Large numbers settled in the area when they were burned out of the City during the Great Fire of London. French Protestants found refuge here following the revocation of the Edict of Nantes in 1685 and recently there has been a huge influx of the famine-starved Irish.

By the middle of the nineteenth century, London's population has soared. In *London, A Social History*, Roy Porter notes that 'Between 1841 and 1851 alone, some 330,000 migrants flooded into the capital, representing a staggering 17% of London's total population. Of these,

46,000 came from Ireland...swelling the London Irish community to around 130,000. In the 1850s a further 286,000 migrants arrived; in the 1860s, 331,000'. London is experiencing a population explosion and a disproportionately high number of these immigrants are finishing up packed into the narrow streets and crowded houses of St Giles.

Some fine houses were built in St Giles during the time of Elizabeth I, a side-effect of her prohibition of new building in the City of London's suburbs. Gradually though, these houses and this district have been abandoned as those who could, moved away from the cramped, foetid and unhealthy inner city areas. Many of the streets themselves are gone, destroyed to allow the construction of New Oxford Street. The formerly grand Elizabethan dwellings have been left to neglect, decay and the depredations of thieves. Some are now only shells, having been stripped of anything of value – doors, window frames, balustrades and metal fittings – and yet these same edifices may now house whole families in each of their cold and bare rooms. People still make money from them. A house let for £25 may be sublet in rooms for £90, and these rooms further sublet until the revenue from the house is £120.

These days St Giles is a quieter, more peaceable place than it was before the new road forced improvements and closed down many of its less salubrious establishments. Twenty years before Mayhew visited, it was a maze of narrow streets and filthy yards and known as a haunt of thieves. Its reputation may have been unfair on the costermongers and hawkers still trying to make an honest living, but in the opinion of police it was well-deserved. Officers would think twice about following felons into St Giles's warren of alleys and courts, which offered every chance of escape for the pursued and dangers for the pursuer.

Mr Hunt, the district's inspector of lodging houses, knows its secrets well. "The houses in Jones Court were connected by roof, yard and cellar with those in Bainbridge and Buckeridge Streets, and with each other in such a manner that the apprehension of an inmate or refugee in one of them was almost a task of impossibility to a stranger and difficult to those well-acquainted with the interior of the dwellings", he says. "In one of the cellars was a cess-pool, covered in such a way that a stranger would likely step into it. In the same cellar was a hole about two feet square, leading to the next cellar and thence by a similar hole into the cellar of a house in Scott's Court, Buckeridge Street. These afforded a ready means of escape to a thief, but effectually stopped the pursuer, who would be put to the risk of creeping on his hands and knees through a hole two feet square in a dark cellar in St Giles' Rookery, entirely in the power of dangerous characters". Such was the importance placed on ready means of egress from the rookery that "in some instances there was a communication from one back window to another by means of large spike nails, one row to hold by and another for the feet to rest on".

Hunt paints a vivid picture of the recreational amenities afforded by the area. The Rose and Crown, for instance, is:

> resorted to by all classes of the light-fingered gentry, from the mobsman and his 'Amelia' to the lowest of the street thieves and his 'Poll'. In the tap room might be seen Black Charlie the fiddler with ten or a dozen lads and lasses enjoying the dance and singing and smoking over potations of gin-and-water, more or less plentiful according to the proceeds of the previous night – all apparently free from care in their wild carousals. Cheeks waxed pale when the policeman opened the door and glanced round the room but when he departed the merriment would be resumed with vigour.

St Giles is still a slum area and the home of the desperate, and sometimes of the dangerous. Here, as in Whitechapel, Shoreditch, the Ratcliffe Highway and other places where survival is a struggle, many of the children seen "fluttering in rags" are taking their first steps in criminal careers that may one day get them imprisoned, transported, or worse. These "street arabs" are to be seen "in vast shoals" at the street markets, loitering with clear intent by shops whose wares are displayed in the street and doorway and prowling in districts in which

14

it might be possible to steal fruit and comestibles from costermongers' barrows, knock a female stall-holder from her seat and snatch the few pennies on her counter, take trinkets from a tray or play on the sympathies of anyone who might be parted from some loose change.

Some children have been sent out to steal – often at the tender age of only six or seven – and some are hungry, while others are egged on by their mischievous friends. Few can read or write – Forster's Education Act, which will make the education of five to twelve year olds compulsory, won't become law until 1870. In the meantime, destitute children might, if they are lucky, receive the bare bones of an education at a Ragged School, or perhaps from one of a handful of high-minded private individuals who have taken it upon themselves to share their learning in places where it is clearly needed.

Many of the crimes committed by these street kids are quite artful. Shopkeepers may find themselves robbed after a cap has been thrown into their doorway. A child will follow the cap and, if the shopman is absent or distracted, then steal his goods or rifle his till; if he is challenged, the child will claim that another boy standing outside threw in his cap as a jape and he is only retrieving it. Another dodge practised by these nascent criminals is 'star-glazing', in which a hole is cut in the glass of a shop window and the goods on display are snatched by the handful. Mayhew paints a vivid picture:

> *In the dark winter evenings we can sometimes see groups of these ragged boys, assembled around the windows of a small grocery-shop, looking greedily at the almond-rock, lollipops, sugar-candy, barley-sugar, brandy-balls, pies and tarts displayed in all their tempting sweetness…They insert the point of a knife…into the corner or side of the pane, then give it a wrench…the pane cracks in a semi-circular, star-like form around the part punctured…The thief inserts his hand…seizes a handful of sweets or other goods and runs away, perhaps followed by the shopman in full chase.*

15

Generally unwashed, the street arabs wear a motley assortment of clothes – which may have come from the 'slop' shops of Seven Dials, where often filthy, second and third-hand clothes are retailed. Garments may also have been handed on by older children or, of course, stolen. Mayhew reports seeing boys without jackets, caps or shoes, others wearing an "old tattered coat, much too large for them," an "old jacket rent at the elbows" or "ragged trousers hung by one brace". Older children who dress a little better are often those who have started to make a career of crime. Then there are the fully-fledged pickpockets of the 'swell mob', who dress "in the highest style of fashion, glittering in gold chains, studs and rings". For the child with only one brace, the impulse to better himself through similar means must have been all but irresistible.

An example of how much importance professional pickpockets placed on correct dress is provided by a policeman interviewed by Henry Mayhew. He reports that while on duty at the Cremorne pleasure gardens in Chelsea, he "observed a man, a boy and a woman, whom he suspected to be picking pockets. The man was about 28 years of age, rather under the middle size". The woman hovering at his side was very good looking, "about 24 years of age and dressed in a green-coloured gown, Paisley shawl and straw bonnet trimmed with red velvet and red flowers. The man wore a black frock coat, brown trousers and black hat", while the boy was dressed in a "brown shooting coat, corduroy trousers and black cap with peak".

They might be a happy family enjoying an evening of diversion at the pleasure gardens. But then the officer "observed the man touch the boy on the shoulder and point him towards an old lady. The boy placed himself on her right side, and the man and the woman kept behind. The former put his left hand into the pocket of the lady's gown and drew nothing from it and then left her and went about two yards farther; there he placed himself by two other ladies, tried both their pockets and left them again. He followed another lady and succeeded in picking her pocket of a small sum of money and a handkerchief".

Pickpockets often are taught their skills by their companions, though Mayhew makes mention of Fagin-like thief trainers and describes their methods: "A coat is suspended on the wall, with a bell attached to it and the boy attempts to take the handkerchief from the pocket without the bell ringing. Until he is able to do this with proficiency, he is not considered well-trained. Another way in which they are trained is this: the trainer walks up and down the room with a handkerchief in the tail of his coat and the ragged boys amuse themselves abstracting it until they learn to do it in an adroit manner". Fagin did much the same and, like Dickens's monster, the boys are sent out to steal for him. "The base wretches buy the handkerchiefs from the boys at a paltry sum", we are told.

When they are not watching for opportunities in the streets, the children might be found spending their ill-gotten income at a beer shop or at one of the 'penny gaff' theatres, where they will see a robust programme of licentious humour and bawdy songs sung by scantily-dressed Cockney chanteuses. Without education and often without provision for their daily bread, with adults who may encourage or even teach them to steal, and flashily-dressed thieves as their role-models, it's hardly surprising that such a large proportion of these children fall into a life of crime and that for many their speciality will be pickpocketing.

There is a market for almost everything and somewhere there is always a thief who will steal it. Even the clothes on children's backs aren't safe, especially if they have value. *Child stripping* is "generally done by two females...who watch their opportunity to accost children in the street, tidily dressed in good boots and clothes". The women entice their victim into a quiet place and strip him of his clothes. Laundry is no safer. Sheets, counterpanes, shirts, pinafores and tablecloths left out to dry are stolen by thieves known colloquially as *snow-gatherers.*

Children despatched to deliver washing are accosted in a similar manner, sometimes being sent into a shop to buy themselves something sweet while a stranger kindly minds their bundle. All of these items can quickly be disposed of at disreputable 'dolly shops', pawn shops which effectively double as fences for stolen goods.

Up the Spout: a visit to the pawn shop

For working-class families living in the poorer districts of mid-century London, the pawn shop is a regular resort. Visits to 'Uncle', as pawnbrokers are euphemistically called, to put something 'up the spout' are common. Small amounts of money are borrowed to buy food, fuel or, too often, drink. Household items or clothing are left as security, either to be redeemed when the borrower has cash, or to be sold by the pawnbroker. Buying the item back usually means paying an additional five per cent of the sum borrowed.

By mid-century, there are around 400 pawnbroking establishments in London alone and borrowing in this way has become the norm, despite various alternatives, as Jerry White points out in *London In The Nineteenth Century: A Human Awful Wonder of God* (2007): 'building societies...savings or loans clubs based on trades unions and church missions and co-operative societies, and the more risky local versions that mushroomed in pubs and working men's clubs'.

Charles Dickens isn't impressed. Adopting the portentous tone of his more serious *Sketches by Boz*, he comments: 'Of the numerous receptacles for misery and distress with which the streets of London unhappily abound, there are, perhaps, none which present such striking scenes as the pawnbrokers' shops. The very nature and description of these places occasions their being but little known, except to the unfortunate beings whose profligacy or misfortune drives them to seek the temporary relief they offer'.

It's not only the working-classes who hock their valuables, he says, noting that 'there are grades of pawning as in everything else'. The better sort of pawnbroker, Dickens reveals, 'calls himself a silversmith and decorates his shop with handsome trinkets and expensive jewellery'. This sort is discreet about what he does, while 'the more humble money-lender boldly advertises his calling and invites observation'.

When Dickens decides to inspect one of the latter kind, he finds what he wants near Drury Lane, adjacent to a gin shop. The pawnshop he selects offers discretion of another sort. There is, Dickens observes, 'a side entrance for the accommodation of such customers as may be desirous of avoiding the observation of the passers-by, or the chance of recognition in a public street'. He describes the place as 'a low, dirty-looking, dusty shop, the door of which stands always doubtfully a little way open, half inviting, half repelling the hesitating visitor, who, if he be as yet uninitiated, examines one of the old garnet brooches in the window for a minute or two with affected eagerness, as if he contemplated making a purchase and then, looking cautiously around to ascertain that no-one watches him, hastily slinks in'.

The shop's windows are crammed with a motley selection of 'old china cups, some modern vases...several sets of chessmen, two or three flutes, a few fiddles...some gaudily-bound prayer books...two rows of silver watches, tea spoons, rings, penholders, snuff boxes, silk and cotton handkerchiefs, carpenters' tools, and wearing apparel of every description'. The side door, he says, 'opens into a small passage from which some half-dozen doors (which may be secured on the inside by bolts) open into a corresponding number of little dens, or closets, which face the counter'. As usual, Dickens collects human detail, noting the 'old, sallow-looking woman' who carries a bundle and interrupts the conversation of the clerks behind the counter. "Now, Mr Henry, do make haste", she urges him, "for my two grandchildren's locked up at home and I'm afeer'd of the fire".

Some pawnshops are fronts for fences of stolen goods and the handkerchiefs on sale here may well be booty sold on by pickpockets. The clothes, which have probably been coming in and out of the shop for years, steadily decreasing in value, eventually become the apparel of the neediest and are known sources of disease. The shops offer pitiful remuneration to their distressed customers, who may have little choice when work is scarce or health fails. Sometimes the choice is between this and crime.

Opportunities for the sneak thief are everywhere, and especially at the railway stations, where carts and wagons queue to receive goods from the trains. These robberies may be done with the connivance of the carters: according to Mayhew, carters may take thieves along to assist with the work and "when an opportunity occurs, carry off…bales of bacon, cheese, bags of nails, boxes of tin and copper and travellers' luggage, which they dispose of to marine-store dealers". In London, valuables are forever falling off the backs of carts.

Lead is stolen from the roofs of houses, especially from those under repair and often by the workmen themselves, who may strip neighbouring houses of lead while they repair another. There is a ready market for planes, saws, squares and hammers as well as for building materials. Outhouses are vulnerable, especially if they house the washing copper. Incredibly, daring robberies from moving cabs and carriages are not unknown. In these cases, the would-be robbers "follow the vehicle with a horse and cart…two or three thieves generally in the cart". With the driver of the target vehicle sitting in front, one of the thieves "pulls down a trunk or box and slips it into the cart, then drives away with the booty".

So many of the crimes seem so paltry and the sentences so disproportionately heavy, especially in the cases of children. In David T. Hawkins's comprehensive *Criminal Ancestors, A Guide to Historical Records in England and Wales*, we are introduced to four young offenders, all photographed for their police records. In 1871, 11-year-old William Watts has a heavy brow and an anxious expression. For stealing 20 ploughshares, William received one month's hard labour. Mary Ann Barber, 12, stole a hat and a pair of boots. She sits prim and erect for the long exposure. Her hair is clean and brushed and parted in the middle. She sits with her lands clasped on her lap, with no idea that her crime will earn her a month's hard labour and then *five years* in Doncaster's reformatory school.

Hannah Martin looks coyly away from the lens and appears much younger than her 12 years. In 1870 she posed in expensive-looking clothes, before being sentenced to three months in prison for stealing 7s 6d. George Davey, 10, was imprisoned for 'one month with hard labour' for stealing two tame rabbits, but 11 year old James Leadbetter got off lightly: his sentence was a mere four days – for stealing celery. Then there is a 13-year-old Birmingham boy with flyaway hair and a Jack the lad look, who, in 1871, landed 21 days hard labour for simple larceny. He stares you out from down the years. On the chalk board resting on his knee is his name, Charles Henry Edward Twist.

Thirteen-year-old Thomas Groves got seven years in Parkhurst for 'stealing wearing apparel'. Perhaps this took into account the opinion, recorded on the Millbank Prison Male Register, that he 'is supposed to have lived in crime about five years' and that he was 'once imprisoned for having lodged in an outhouse.' It sounds very much like he had nowhere else to go and perhaps no other direction open to him than a criminal one. The report adds, 'was left when an infant at the door of a house in Whitechapel'.

Not everyone, as we will see, makes a good pickpocket. The best are sharp-minded individuals who can spot an opportunity, as well as accurately gauge their chances of getting away with it, and they must, of course, be manually dextrous. To slip a hand among crinolines, cut away a pocket or take a breast-chain pocket watch without the notice of your victim takes skill and lots of practise.

But if you are clumsy and still inclined towards crime, then other opportunities abound in this thriving metropolis. You might, for instance, become a *sneak thief.* Mayhew and his contemporaries had a pigeon-hole for everyone and even this category spawns others: "There are various orders of Sneak", Mayhew says, "from the urchin stealing an apple at a stall to the man who enters a dwelling by the area or an attic window and carries off the silver plate". A sneak thief is a cunning opportunist, always waiting his chance to slip away with anything of value not locked up or nailed down.

The Abingdon-born sneak Mayhew spoke to is described as 'a poor wretched creature…of feeble intellect and worthless character'. Like Dick, the man we'll call Toby was met in a low lodging house. At 14, Toby was, according to his own account, "a steady, well-conducted boy" who could read, if not write. After his father died, he spent three years working with his uncle, a basket-maker and rag merchant, but when the work dried up, he went travelling with a 'Cheap Jack', an itinerant seller of assorted dry goods, handing out purchases to buyers in the markets. Toby doesn't say why he started stealing, but at a fair in Reading, he comes across a sleeping drunk and pilfers his boots and handkerchief. The same day, he is able to pawn the boots at Windsor for three shillings and the handkerchief for one shilling.

Dumping the hard and precarious life of a Cheap Jack's assistant, Toby heads for London, where he lives in seedy lodging houses and tries to make a living as a street singer of popular ballads such as 'The Dark-eyed Sailor' and the dubious-sounding 'The Female Cabin Boy'. Competition would have been stiff; at almost any corner, the refrain of the ballad singer would compete not only with other ballad singers but with the street cries of "potatoes, all 'ot!" and "fresh herrings!" He tries to augment the money he earns from singing ballads and doing odd jobs with pickpocketing, but he's not very good at it. "In the course of our interview," Henry Mayhew says, "we saw he was very clumsy at picking pockets", though whether Toby was demonstrating or trying to pick the pockets of Mayhew and his guide isn't clear.

Toby lives a down-at-heel and hopeless existence enlivened by the sort of reading matter widely popular among the fraternity of thieves. Books about famous criminals like Jack Shepherd and Dick Turpin find a ready readership in the low lodging houses, as does the perennially popular *Newgate Calendar*. (The book that Fagin offers Oliver Twist to read, a "history of the lives and trials of great criminals", is very probably the *Newgate Calendar*.) According to Toby, the lodging houses are full of sneak thieves, who tend to go out on the streets in pairs. "One of them keeps a look-out while the other steals some article, shoes, vest or a coat etc, from the shop or stall. I sometimes go out with a mate and take a pair of boots at a shop door and sell them to the pawnbroker or to a labouring man passing in the street".

The sneak thieves have their little dodges, too, like the one Toby describes here: "Sometimes I have known the lodgers make up a packet of sawdust and put a little piece of tobacco to cover an opening...and sell it to persons passing by in the street as a packet of tobacco". More usually, the sneak thieves are on the lookout for items like the silver snuff box which Toby succeeded in stealing from a man's coat pocket (perhaps he wasn't wearing it) or the pocket book he pilfered, which contained postage stamps to the value of 1s 6d. He steals loaves of bread, handkerchiefs, quart pots and anything he can get his hands on.

It's all small beer and although he picks pockets when he can, he's not sufficiently successful to pick the type of pockets that might contain something valuable. "I never had clothes respectable enough to try purses and watches", he says. Nor, he admits, did he have the nerve for it. It's easy to see why Toby is at the bottom of the thieves' pecking order; pickpockets above him and skilled burglars at the top.

Dognappers

Even dogs aren't safe in Victorian London, especially, Mayhew notes, those dogs "ladies are fond of – spaniels, poodles and terriers, sporting dogs such as setters and retrievers and also Newfoundlands". Having exhausted his list of dogs at risk, Mayhew describes the *modus operandi* of the typical dog thief: "When they see a handsome dog with a lady or gentleman, they follow it and see where the person resides". They then "loiter about the house for days with a piece of liver prepared by a certain process and soaked in some ingredient which dogs are uncommonly fond of. They are so partial to it they will follow the stranger some distance".

Bitches in heat are also used to decoy unwary dogs: "When a valuable dog follows, it is picked up and taken home", where the dognappers wait for a reward to be offered for its return. The owner is told the dog will be returned for "a certain sum of money, if not, it will be killed". Some dogs, Mayhew says, "are stolen three or four times". Just as pickpockets have their fences, so the dog stealers have 'dog receivers' or 'dog fanciers', men who will return the dog for a part of the reward. "Dogs are frequently restored by agencies of this description", Mayhew says. Like today's high-end cars today, "Some of those stolen are sent to Germany, where English dogs are sold at a high price".

Dickens's Bill Sykes is a burglar and the sort of monstrous villain who will stop at nothing to feed his appetites. He's a criminal through and through, and is described as having the kind of legs 'which always look in an unfinished and incomplete state without a set of fetters to garnish them'. He goes on his burglaries armed, drunk and sometimes with a terrified child in tow. Small children came in handy for slipping through fanlights and windows to open doors. If Sykes gains respect, it's on account of his terrifying presence and not for the cunning and skills which have earned other burglars their place at the top of the criminal tree.

The industrious Victorian in Mayhew seems almost to admire the skilled burglar: "In manual adroitness", he says, the burglar "equals the accomplished pickpocket". Mayhew gains the trust of several. He doesn't name them and doubtless that suits them too, but Mayhew also sees his subjects as types, rather than as individuals. He imposes terms and invents taxonomies for everything, which is very contemporary and scientific, but means that most of his interviewees' names are invented.

'Tom' is a returned convict. Before being transported to Australia, he enjoyed a profitable career as someone who kept watch while other gang members committed burglaries. He is a "slim-made man" of "beneath middle size", Mayhew says, "with a keen, dark, intelligent eye and about 36 years of age. He is good-looking….and in the attire of a well-dressed mechanic". Tom was born in 1825 to a coach and harness maker and a milliner, the youngest but two of 11 children. His father dies when he is eight, and at nine he is sent out to work.

After making a promising start, Tom is led astray by an elder brother, who encourages him to steal from a succession of mostly generous employers. Out of work, he begins cutting the strings of ladies' reticules – draw-string purses carried on the waist – and shoplifting from stationers' shops, where he steals "silver pencil cases, silver and gold mounted scent-bottles and other articles". Being well-dressed, he says, he could enter a shop and pretend to "price an article of jewellery or such like valuable". After getting it in his hand, he would "dart out the shop with it".

It is a stage performance of the ever-popular *Jack Shepherd* that persuades Tom to turn to burglary. Philip Scott, an old schoolfriend of

Tom's newly returned from the sea, tells him of a place in the City where they might steal silver plate and, armed with a screwdriver and a knife, they go out one night to burgle it. Assisted by Tom, Philip gets over a wall at the back of the house, using his knife to free the catch of a window. "He had not been in above three quarters of an hour when he handed me a silver pot and cream jug from the wall", Tom tells Mayhew. "I conveyed these to the coffee shop in which we lodged and we afterwards disposed of them".

After burgling a private house in which their booty comprises of more silver plate along with "three shirts, two coats and an umbrella", they are disturbed while robbing a house in the City. When Philip is jailed, Tom is persuaded to join with two more confederates, who are planning a raid on a West End shop. "There happened to be a dog in the shop", Tom says. "As soon as they got in, the dog barked. They cut the dog's throat with a knife and began to plunder the shop of pencil cases, scent bottles, postage stamps etc". They took the property to a receiver of stolen goods and got £42 for it. After a string of similar crimes, "in the year 1851", he says, "I was transported…for burglary. I returned home on a ticket of leave [*probationary release*] in 1854 and was sent back the following year for harbouring an escaped convict. I returned home in 1858, at the expiry of my sentence and since that time have abandoned my former criminal life".

Burglars effect their entries in numerous ingenious ways. If the padlock on the door to a warehouse is broken, a copy of the padlock may be used to give the impression to a policeman on the beat that all is well within. Door panels may be removed, holes made in floors from rooms above and entry effected through the roof. A common ploy for burglars is to enter another, possibly unoccupied house in the row and make their way towards their target along the attic roof space. Servants are courted or bribed to provide impressions of keys or to supply information about a house and the habits of its residents. Lights in windows are watched for the same reason.

A member of a gang may secrete himself on the premises and let in his mates when the coast is clear. Lookouts and decoys are used to obstruct policemen. A female gang member called a *canary* may be used not only to carry tools (a woman being less likely to be challenged) but to distract interested parties from the scene of the robbery. The woman may walk the street outside "as though she were a common prostitute", Mayhew says, adding that when the necessity arises, she may familiarly accost the policeman and lure him away, but if this doesn't work she may pretend to fall down in a fit, obliging the policeman to take her "to the nearest surgeon".

While opportunistic burglars will open a house with whatever is to hand, the professional favours specialised tools. According to Mayhew, a well-prepared burglar may have at his disposal "a jemmy, a cutter, a dozen picklocks, a jack to remove iron bars, a dark lantern [a lamp with a sliding shutter to restrict light] or a taper...and a life-preserver". He may also carry a rope and knives and chisels for breaking open desk drawers. Stolen goods may be carried off by a cart or cab, whose driver is loitering in a nearby street. "Lighter goods such as jewellery", Mayhew says, "are generally taken away in carpet-bags in time to catch an early train". The robbers being respectably dressed, they often pass policemen unchallenged, looking like men of business with trains to catch.

Some burglars are surprisingly agile. Constables suspecting a burglary is in progress in "a large linen-drapery establishment in the Westminster Road" discover that thieves have entered the shop by scaling a drainpipe and walking along a high wall before opening a skylight and letting themselves down into the shop by means of a rope ladder. On being disturbed, the thieves jump from one house to another. The houses are eight feet apart and their roofs 50 feet above the pavement.

Sometimes they are not agile enough. In 1850, a furrier's on the corner of Regent Street is broken into by Henry Edgar (who, we're told, was about 5ft 7in and dressed in an elegant, gentlemanly style) and by his accomplice, Edward Edgar Blackwell (5ft 2in, fashionably dressed but with a sullen look). A third person isn't named, but we are told instead that he is of slim build, with dark whiskers and a genteel appearance. Between ten and eleven o'clock, two of these men leave the bar of a pub "with the pretence of going to the water closet". They aren't missed and by means of the fire escape, climb over the parapet of the furrier's, cutting through the panes in a garret window – where they are immediately discovered by a servant, who was going to bed in the dark. We are told that the girl gives no alarm, but goes downstairs, where she alerts her master. "The master came up and, with two loaded pistols in his hand" warns the intruders that if they attempt to escape, he will shoot them.

Edward Edgar Blackwell is so frightened that he loses "his presence of mind" and falls from the parapet into the yard, a height of three storeys, and is killed on the spot. Henry Edgar makes a desperate leap from the parapet to a house in Regent Street and climbs through a trapdoor to get into the house itself. Alarming people who were sleeping in the second floor front, he makes a second leap, this from a second-floor window but is quickly arrested and "conveyed in a cab, with the dead body of his pal, to Vine Street police station".

London's crime in figures

In 1853, a report made by the Constabulary Commissioners attempted to gauge the amount of crime and number of criminals then at work in London. 'According to this', John Binny writes, 'there were in the Metropolis...107 burglars, 110 housebreakers, 38 highway robbers, 773 pickpockets, 3,657 sneaks-men or common thieves, 11 horse stealers and 141 dog stealers, three forgers, 28 coiners and 317 utterers of base coin, 141 swindlers and obtainers of goods under false pretences and 182 cheats, 343 receivers of stolen goods, 2,768 habitual rioters, 1,205 vagrants, 50 begging letter writers, 86 bearers of begging letters, 6,371 prostitutes', and a further 470 'not otherwise described'. This, he says, gives 'a total of 16,900 criminals known to the police, so it would appear that one in every 140 of the London population belongs to the criminal class'.

Property made away with by this enterprising section of society amounts, Binny says, to 'very nearly £42,000 per annum'.

Another dextrous burglar is Gerry, 32, a slim, fair complexioned man of about 5ft 2in , with "a keen grey eye". He's reputed to be "one of the most daring thieves in the metropolis". When Mayhew meets him, he is wearing dark trousers, brown vest and a grey frock-coat buttoned up to the chin. A cap is drawn over his eyes. At first Mayhew wonders whether this little man is capable of the cat burglaries said to be his speciality, but then "he led us along a dark street to an adjoining back court, took off his shoes and stockings and ran up a waterspout to the top of a lofty house and slid down again with surprising agility".

Born in St Giles to Irish parents, two of Gerry's sisters have been transported for stealing watches and another, "lately come out of prison after 18 months" is now living honestly. Sent out to sell oranges in the street at the age of 10, Gerry falls into bad company and like Dick, joins the boys sleeping under the Adelphi arches, where he too learns to pick pockets. At 17, after an introductory stretch in Brixton Prison, he shacks up with a prostitute (handsome, kind-hearted, inclined to be stout). She had not been with him long when he falls in with a pair of burglars and together, they break into a counting house in the West End. It doesn't go well.

"At one o' clock in the morning", he says, "one of the party was set to watch in the street to give us the signal when no-one was near… I and another climbed up a waterspout to the roof of the counting house. There was no other way of getting in but by cutting the lead off the house and making an opening sufficient for us to pass through. The signal was given to enter the house, but at this time, the policeman saw our shadow on the roof and sprung his rattle". The boy who was keeping watch (not very effectively, it seems) got away and so did the third member of the gang. Gerry, though, hurt himself getting down from the rooftop to the street and some time afterwards, receives a further nine month stretch at Middlesex Assizes.

With a new, "more expert" gang, he robs a shop in the City, which entails climbing over a number of walls to reach the targeted premises. Cutting through a door panel to gain access, they make off with silks (which they sell) and spend the proceeds on "theatres and gambling" and living "very expensively on the best viands, with wines and other liquors". One successful burglary leads to another and a concomitant variety of interesting escapades. He is shot at by one householder and at another house, he finds himself in danger of being discovered by a lady coming upstairs.

Gerry hides himself under a bed "when the lady and her servant came into the room with a light. They closed the door and pulled the curtains down…the lady began to wash her face and neck." He mentions that the lady is "a beautiful creature" and it's clear he's finding his quandary more than a little stimulating: "While lying under the bed," he confides, "I distinctly saw the maid put perfume on the lady's under linen". When the lady has dressed and left the room, Gerry pockets a locket and gold chain, a gold pencil case and a silver thimble, but making his way to "the first floor back" to effect his escape, he is able to add "a case of jewels" to his haul.

Insider information is crucial to the success of burglaries. Employees of the establishment, or tradesmen who have had reason to enter the house legitimately, sell their knowledge at a price. When a pot-man informs Gerry that a large amount of cash is sitting in a public house (the brewer's bill being due), Gerry has to get himself to the first floor of the pub without attracting the notice of the landlady or her daughter. Gerry's cronies start a row in the taproom, allowing Gerry to slip upstairs to search for the cash. Downstairs, the landlady has sent her daughter to fetch a policeman to deal with the trouble in the taproom.

Unfortunately, one of the burglars is known to the constable, who suspects something is up and asks the landlady if anyone else came in with these two men. Now that she thinks about it, the landlady does recall another man. "I was coming downstairs with the cashbox when I heard this conversation", says Gerry. "The constable asked leave to search the house. I ran with the cashbox up the staircase and looked in the back room to see if there was any place to get away, but there was none".

Gerry opens a garret window and gets onto the roof, intending to hide there – but he has left muddy footprints on the carpet and is followed by two policemen. Nimbler than his pursuers, he runs along the roofs of the row of houses and slips down a drainpipe and climbs another to the roof of the stable. Here he lies low until the police change their watch. When eventually he is able to climb down into the stable yard, he is spotted and accosted by the stable man, who cries out, "Here he is!" Gerry says he has no alternative "but to fight for it. I had a jemmy in my pocket. He laid hold of me…I struck him in the face with it and he fell to the ground". Following this, Gerry is a hunted man and has to hole up in the house of a Whitechapel cigar maker until the heat is off.

There is more than a touch of the Bill Sykes about Gerry, a brutal streak which is evident from these episodes. In a Whitechapel pub he's enjoying a glass of rum and water with his pal, "a tall, athletic young fellow of about 19 years, handsomely dressed with gold ring and pin". His pal, he says, is "intelligent and daring". At the bar is a recruiting sergeant "belonging to a company in the line" who invites the pair to drink with him. Taking the King's shilling but giving false names and addresses, they try but fail to fleece the sergeant at bagatelle. When he leaves them, heading in the direction of the barracks at Hyde Park, they follow him, Gerry's pal swearing "we shall not leave him till we have plundered him". Gerry, who tries to mitigate his crime by claiming to have been the worse for liquor, offers to garotte the sergeant, if his pal will help.

What happens next is a good example of the sort of mugging frightening Londoners to the extent that it is even possible to buy a spiked 'garotte-proof collar'. Gerry describes the attack: "I sprang upon his neck. Being a stronger man than I, he struggled violently. I kept hold of him until he became senseless". They rob him of pocket-book, papers, a watch and chain and some gold coins. There's further violence when the two men quarrel with skittle-sharps, one of whom annoys Gerry's partner sufficiently to earn himself a sharp blow from a life-preserver. They rob a gentleman relieving "a poor crossing sweeper with a piece of silver" and violently resist arrest.

It's suggested by a female servant that they rob the neighbouring house to her employer's, where a surgeon is often on call in the evenings. Gerry hides under a sofa when the surgeon returns home unexpectedly. As the doctor is taking off his boots, he sees one of Gerry's shoeless feet, protruding from under his seat. Grabbing hold of Gerry's leg, he "dragged me from under the sofa. He was a strong man and kneeled on my back...I gave a signal to my companion behind him, who struck him a violent blow on the back...which felled him to the floor". The surgeon chases them down the street, Gerry in his bare feet. "Our female friend had the presence of mind...to run into the house and get my boots", Gerry says. After carrying them into her employer's house, the girl covers her tracks by raising the alarm and shouting "thieves!"

Gerry was transported twice and reckons that all told, he has spent 14 years behind bars – almost half of his 32 years.

But the Victorian burglar who – despite his expressed wish to be forgotten after his death – is still remembered, is Sheffield-born Charley Peace. Although convicted and executed for murder, there is something about this energetic and purposeful thief which prevents him from being assigned to the company of the murderers we'll meet later. If nothing else, the sheer number of his burglaries should earn him a place within this chapter. Born Charles Frederick Peace in 1832 to respectable parents (his father was a collier-turned-animal trainer, his mother the daughter of a naval surgeon), Charles attends two schools near Sheffield, where his restless energy finds expression in the making of paper models and peep-shows, the taming of cats and an ability to catch a heavy ball of shot in a leather socket fixed to his forehead.

Leaving school, Charles finds work at a steel rolling mill but in 1846, he is injured in an industrial accident. Red-hot steel pierces his leg below the knee, obliging him to spend the next 18 months in the Sheffield Infirmary, which he leaves with a pronounced limp. At around this time, Peace's father dies and his passing is marked, as are so many other Peace family events, with a line of verse:

In peace he lived; In peace he died; Life was our desire,
but God denied.

31

Why Peace starts out on a life of crime isn't recorded. It might be that he falls in with a bad crowd, or accrues debts, but it seems as likely that the adrenaline-fuelled life of a burglar is well-suited to his temperament. Stealing a gentleman's gold watch is thought to be his first crime, but in 1851, he enters the house of a lady living in Sheffield and makes off with property which is later found in his possession. Because of a good character reference from an employer, Peace receives a lenient sentence of one month's imprisonment. It's after this that we hear of his other talents, of which music is one. Those who hear him play the one-stringed violin dub him a "modern Paganini" and, later in his life, when he lives in a suburban villa at Peckham, he will collect a harmonium, guitars, banjos and violins.

However, a spell in prison doesn't dull his taste for excitement and Peace is soon honing his burgling skills and despite the disability caused by his accident, is becoming known as a "portico thief", a burglar who effects entry into premises by means of the house's portico. In 1854 Peace is again arrested, and sentenced to four years imprisonment. His sister, who is found in possession of stolen goods, gets six months. Her death, shortly after she is freed, is the occasion of another line of questionable verse, probably penned by Peace himself:

> *I was so long apprest* [sic]
> *That wore my strength away;*
> *It made me long for endless rest*
> *Which never can decay.*

When he is released in 1858, Peace extends his operations as far as Manchester, and after breaking into a house there, buries his booty in a field, where it is discovered the next day. Police lie in wait and spring their trap and, says H.B. Irving in *The Life of Charles Peace* (1918), 'after nearly killing the officer who was trying to arrest him, would have made his escape, had not another policeman come to his rescue'. This earns Peace a further six years behind bars, 'in spite of a loyal act of perjury on the part of his aged mother, who came all the way from Sheffield to swear that he had been with her on the night of his crime'.

Peace receives another eight years for a burglary committed in 1866, and it is during this last stretch that he attempts a daring escape from Wakefield prison. Working on some repairs, Peace is able to smuggle a small ladder into his cell. Having already made a saw from tin, he cuts a hole in the roof of his cell and is about to get out onto the roof when a warder enters. Peace fights off the warder and makes it onto the roof of the prison, where he runs along the wall before falling off on the wrong side. He is still able to enter the governor's house, where he changes his clothes and waits for a chance to escape. He is recaptured in the governor's bedroom. Despite his advancing years, this isn't the last Peace will see of prison. Penitentiaries at Millbank, Chatham and Gibraltar all open their gates for him before his final release in 1872.

In 1859, Peace marries Hannah Ward, a woman who already had a son and during his fourth prison term, bears him a son, who dies before his father's release and is commemorated with these words:

Farewell my dear son, by all us beloved.
Thou art gone to dwell in the mansions above.
In the bosom of Jesus Who sits on the throne
Thou art anxiously waiting to welcome us home.

Peace, who is said to have been able to turn his hand to most things, now becomes a picture framer. He plies his trade and sends his children to Sunday school, and in 1875, he and his family move to the Sheffield suburb of Darnall, where, fatally, he makes the acquaintance of a Mr and Mrs Dyson, who have recently returned from America. The precise nature of the relationship between Charles Peace and Mrs Dyson is never established. Before his execution, Peace assures the Vicar of Darnell that Mrs Dyson had been his mistress, a state of affairs always strenuously denied by the lady herself. What the 25-year-old 'buxom and blooming' woman could have seen in the unquestionably ugly Peace is hard to see, but evidence presented backing up Peace's claim includes a photograph of them together, a ring he had given her and reports of the two attending music halls and visiting pubs in each other's company.

In the early summer of 1876, Mr Dyson decides to do something about Peace's intrusion into his marriage and throws a card into Peace's garden, on which is written 'Charles Peace is requested not to interfere with my family'. Perhaps as a consequence, Peace tries to trip up Dyson in the street. Later that same day, he finds Mrs Dyson chatting with friends and threatens "in coarse and violent language to blow out her brains and those of her husband". Dyson then takes out a summons against Peace, who quickly decamps to Hull, where his wife opens an eating shop. From Hull, Peace goes to Manchester again and, while burgling a house, commits his first murder. Seen by two policemen as he enters a house in Whalley Range, he is tackled by Constable Cock as he tries to escape.

> *Peace took out his revolver and warned Cock to stand back. The policeman came on. Peace fired, but deliberately wide of him. Cock, undismayed, drew out his truncheon, and made for the burglar. Peace, desperate, determined not to be caught, fired again, this time fatally. Cock's comrade heard the shots, but before he could reach the side of the dying man, Peace had made off. He returned to Hull, and there learned shortly after, to his intense relief, that two brothers, John and William Habron, living near the scene of the murder, had been arrested and charged with the killing of Constable Cock.*

Meanwhile, the Dysons move to another Sheffield suburb. No doubt Dyson thinks that in Banner Cross, they will be able to forget about Charles Peace and get on with their lives, but the family have no sooner moved in than Dyson encounters Peace in the neighbourhood of the house. Peace makes it clear that his campaign of harassment is far from over. "You see", he tells Dyson, "I am here to annoy you and I'll annoy you wherever you go". On another occasion, Peace sees

Dyson in the street and brandishes his revolver, telling the man with him, "If he offers to come near me, I will make him stand back". H.B. Irving suggests as Peace's motives passion, jealousy, spite or revenge and reminds his readers that by procuring a warrant, Dyson had driven Peace from his Sheffield home. Whatever his motives, Peace became irritable, occasionally violent and obsessed with the Dysons.

The trial of John and William Habron for the murder of Constable Cock provides him with distraction. Peace attends the trial, which he must witness with an interesting mixture of emotions as John Habron is acquitted while his brother is sentenced to death. As motives, the brothers' previous dealings with Constable Cock are cited (Cock had taken out summonses against the men for being drunk and disorderly) along with their reported threats to "do for him". Two days before the day set for his execution, William Habron is granted a respite by the Home Secretary and his death sentence is later commuted to one of life imprisonment. Peace has got away with murder.

But the Dysons aren't to be let off so easily. On the morning of 28 November, 1876, Peace presents himself at the Dysons' house, telling Mrs Dyson and her mother that he is in Sheffield for the fair. He spends the afternoon of that day in a pub, entertaining customers and earning himself drinks by playing tunes on a poker suspended by a string, which he beats with a short stick. Just after eight pm that evening, Peace positions himself in a passageway behind the terrace in which the Dysons live. He has been there perhaps an hour when he sees Mrs Dyson cross the yard and enter an outhouse. When she comes out, she finds herself looking down the barrel of Peace's revolver. "Speak, or I'll fire", Peace says, but before she can say anything, Mr Dyson comes out to investigate the noise. Peace retreats to the passage and when he sees Dyson following, he fires a shot, which strikes the lintel of the passage doorway. His second shot hits Dyson in the head. Leaving his victim dying, Peace crosses the city and makes for Attercliffe Railway Station, where be buys a ticket for Beverley, but thinking he sees something suspicious in the rail clerk's manner, he gets off the train at Normanton and goes on to York. Detectives come within a whisker of arresting him at his wife's eating shop in Hull, where he is hiding behind a chimney stack. Disguising himself by dying his hair and wearing spectacles, Peace also changes his appearance using his extraordinary ability to contort his features. In this way, Charles Peace, who now has a £100 reward on his head, is able to zigzag across the country, before ending up in Nottingham, where he is taken in by a receiver of stolen goods called Mrs Adamson.

When Nottingham becomes too hot for him, Peace moves again, this time to London, where he sets himself up in Lambeth as a dealer in musical instruments. Peace is later to be found living in Peckham under the name of Thompson and posing as "a gentleman of independent means with a taste for scientific invention". This is not so far-fetched as it seems. Together with a man called Brion, the nothing if not energetic Peace patents an invention for raising sunken vessels and works on a smoke helmet for firemen and an improved brush for washing railway carriages. At night, however, he goes about his other business, carrying a violin case full of burglar's tools.

He may have become careless. The number of burglaries in Blackheath and adjacent districts is raising suspicions and increasing police vigilance. On 10 October, 1878, a police constable called Robinson sees a light suddenly appear in a back window of a house in Blackheath. Summoning colleagues, who ring the bell at the front, Robinson waits at the back and gives chase to a man he sees leave the house by the dining room window. Peace takes out his revolver and fires three shots, which pass close to Robinson's head. Another shot also misses its mark, but the fifth shot fired by Peace passes through Robinson's arm, just above his elbow. Despite this, the constable manages to bring Peace down, and knock him on the head with his own revolver.

With the help of 'Mrs Thomson', and a policeman who had known Peace in Sheffield, the real identity of the arrested man is discovered and Peace is committed for trial for the attempted murder of Constable Robinson and for the burglary of the house. Though Peace claims he had never intended to kill and that the gun went off too easily, the presiding judge feels duty-bound to remove this career criminal from circulation for life. No sooner has one trial ended than Peace is once again in dock, this time at Sheffield, indicted for the murder of Dyson.

'YOU'VE GOT TO PICK A POCKET OR TWO'

This follows a spectacular escape attempt he makes on the train from London to Sheffield.

Peace departs from King's Cross at 5.15 am in the company of two warders, with whom he is "wilful and troublesome". To make sure Peace has no need to leave train at the stops it makes en route, bags have been provided for him to urinate into, which are to be ejected from the window after use. Just after the train had passed Worksop, and not far from their destination, Peace requests one of the bags. When the window is lowered so the bag can be ejected, Peace throws himself out after it. One of the warders catching him by the ankle, Peace is left hanging upside down on the side of a speeding train which the other warder tries to stop by pulling on the communication cord. Peace struggles and manages to free his foot from its shoe and himself falls heavily on the line. When the train eventually stops, Peace is discovered unconscious and bleeding from a head wound.

Despite his injuries, Peace is deemed fit enough to stand trial, which begins a few days later. In his defence, much is made about the attendant publicity – some newspapers have already convicted Peace and his activities both real and those embellished or invented by the press, are eagerly consumed in a variety of published forms. Evidence given by witnesses is shaky – especially that supplied by Mrs Dyson, whose memory of events proves unreliable, to say the least – but even Peace's own counsel seems to doubt that any verdict but one of guilty is possible. Irving reports that:

> Twice, both at the beginning and the end of his speech, Mr. Lockwood urged as a reason for the jury being tender in taking Peace's life that he was in such a state of wickedness as to be quite unprepared to meet death. Both times that his counsel put forward this curious plea, Peace raised his eyes to heaven and exclaimed "I am not fit to die".

It takes the jury only ten minutes to find Peace guilty and the mandatory sentence of death is duly passed. He passes the time

37

between conviction and execution apparently atoning for his life and does at least manage to right one of his wrongs by confessing to the murder of Constable Cock, for which William Habron is serving a life sentence. Of course, Charles Peace couldn't let such an important event as his own death – at Armley prison, on 25 February 1879 – pass without marking it with one final line of verse, which runs:

Lion-hearted I've lived, And when my time comes, Lion-hearted I'll die.

CHAPTER 2

On the Streets
'The lowest class of women'

In the middle of the nineteenth century, if you have blue blood or hard cash, the place to show it off to the world is Rotten Row, on the south side of Hyde Park. Go there any weekend at midday or early evening and you can be sure of seeing Society at play. The upper classes and the fashionable promenade here and make their introductions. They also gossip, but in a very proper way, of course. And on one summer's evening in the early 1860s, no one is attracting more speculation – or drawing more glances – than a striking young lady on horseback, who canters, wheels and kicks up the dirt on a fine thoroughbred. This expert young horsewoman is veiled, but anyone who is anyone knows that this is the infamous 'Skittles', real name Catherine Walters, the most talked-about courtesan in so-called polite society. She canters down the Row, seemingly oblivious of the attention she's attracting. Classically good-looking, with long dark hair in curls and a tight-fitting riding habit in the very latest style (beneath which, it's whispered, she's naked), Skittles is at the top of her game – which is *the* game, of course.

And she must be good at what she does, because not only does she dress so well that respectable ladies follow her fashions, but it seems she can afford to keep a carriage, as reported in an 1862 edition of *The Times*, in an article lightly-disguising Walters as 'Anonyma':

> *Expectation is raised to its highest pitch: a handsome woman drives rapidly by in a carriage drawn by thorough-*

bred ponies of surpassing shape and action; the driver is attired in the pork pie hat and the Poole paletot introduced by Anonyma; but alas!, she caused no effect at all, for she is not Anonyma; she is only the Duchess of A–, the Marchioness of B–, the Countess of C–, or some other of Anonyma's many imitators.

'The crowd, disappointed, reseat themselves, and wait. Another pony carriage succeeds – and another – with the same depressing result. At last their patience is rewarded. Anonyma and her ponies appear, and they are satisfied. She threads her way dexterously, with an unconscious air, through the throng, commented upon by the hundreds who admire and the hundreds who envy her. She pulls up her ponies to speak to an acquaintance, and her carriage is instantly surrounded by a multitude; she turns and drives back again towards Apsley House, and then away into the unknown world, nobody knows whither.

The name of Liverpool-born Skittles, who is said to have earned her sobriquet working in a skittles ground behind Park Lane, is now linked with the great and good of the land. Intellectuals, political leaders, aristocrats and even the Price of Wales, the future King Edward VII, are rumoured to have fallen under her spell. She is a high-class courtesan, the last of the *grandes horizontales*. Her charm, acuity and Scouse-inflected conversation have brought her considerable income and the sort of back-door access to Society her peers can only dream of. Her life is to be a full one, packed with colourful moments – such as her pursuit of the Marquess of Hartington, 8th Duke of Devonshire, to New York during the American Civil War – and when she dies of a cerebral haemorrhage at her Mayfair home in 1920, she will leave a small estate and, they say, further properties in France. For this prostitute at least, the wages of sin will prove ample enough.

But, of course, the career of this extraordinary woman bears no relation at all to that of London's common prostitutes – who are, it seems, everywhere. A police report of 1857 estimates that there are

8,600 working girls in the metropolis. But this figure, according to Henry Mayhew, "scarcely does more than record the circulating harlotry of the Haymarket and Regent Street." Mayhew's own experiences among London's streetwalkers persuades him that even the estimate of Dr Ryan, an expert in this field, falls short of the truth – and Ryan's figure is 80,000.

Whatever the true number of women walking the streets of nineteenth century London, among them are every variation of the oldest profession, from seduced servants finding themselves fit for nothing else and poorly-paid milliners topping up their incomes, to girls looking for easy cash and a good time. There are even married women who prostitute themselves on a part-time basis. Some have become prostitutes after being raped and ruined, while others have gone on the game with their eyes wide open. It should be noted, though, that Mayhew's definition of prostitutes is a widely-cast net, and as well as the plentiful streetwalkers, catches those who operate with more discretion, such as the women who are installed and funded in well-upholstered love nests. Also defined as prostitutes by Mayhew are women kept by sailors on shore leave and soldiers' camp followers. A woman who has been seduced is liable to be lumped in, too.

Although prostitution in itself is not illegal, the crimes it engenders – from the robbery of duped customers and the brutal activities of brothel 'bullies' or doormen to the corruption of innocents and the sheer nuisance this enormous trade causes to people going about their business, more than merits its inclusion here. Some prostitutes are themselves criminals. They may live with thieves and pickpockets and do something in that line themselves or lure drunken or foolish men into quiet streets where they are robbed by accomplices. They are, according to Mayhew, an improvident lot, reckless, shameless and immodest, but capable of acts of generosity too. The common perception of the knots – sometimes small crowds – of girls in fading finery who parade, promenade and loiter in the shopping and theatre districts of the West End is that these are wicked, Godless, 'fallen' women, who will come to a bad end. And this will indeed be the fate of some – the Thames throws up drowned bodies with horrible regularity.

They make various excuses for their way of life. One, when asked about herself, says brazenly, "Oh, I'm a seduced milliner, anything you like", while another changes her story with each telling of it. A kept woman we'll call Molly offers this candid and rather fatalistic view of her lot: "I rather like it. I have all I want and my friend loves me to excess". She says she was seduced four years ago. "I tell you candidly that I was as much to blame as my seducer; I wished to escape the drudgery of my father's shop". With a smattering of education, she thinks she is "qualified for something better" and admits that she was "very fond of dress and could not gratify my love of display".

Since running away to London with her young man, Molly has lived with four men – she is now, to all intents and for Mayhew's purposes, a prostitute – and seems to have no regrets. She says that she keeps her parents "pleasantly aware of my existence by occasionally sending them money". When Mayhew asks her what she thinks may become of her, she dismisses the question as "absurd". I could, she assures him, "marry tomorrow if I liked".

Most prostitutes, says Mayhew, dream of something better. He estimates that girls are usually on the streets for around four years before disappearing, presumably having found an alternative way of making a living. Some women do indeed marry out of the game and there are instances of others setting themselves up in business with the income they've saved. Others, though, are still prostituting themselves when age overtakes them or they contract syphilis. These may continue to live on ever-decreasing incomes or may earn something in one of prostitution's more unusual sidelines.

Followers of dress lodgers are usually older women, often prostitutes who have had their day, who are employed by bawds to keep a close eye on the girls they provide with expensive outfits in order to attract custom. The clothes are loaned to the girl, who pays the bawd part of her earnings. The follower may also be expected to ensure the girl doesn't slack at her soliciting. Other women, whom age and disease have made unfit for anything else, may end up as one of the (sometimes veiled) whores who operate from poorly-lit benches in the London parks. "You may meet them in Hyde Park between the hours of five and ten, when the gates are closed", Mayhew says, adding that "these low wretches" are also to be found in Green Park, walking about "sometimes with men, more generally alone". He describes them "reclining on the benches...occasionally with the head of a drunken man reposing in their lap". These women scrape a frugal living in crepuscular parks, where they may be obliged to give them themselves up to "disgusting practises...gratifying to men of morbid and diseased imaginations".

The park woman Mayhew talks to asks to be rewarded for her trouble. "My time is my money", she tells him, "and I cannot afford to lose either". As the story of her unhappy life unfolds, Mayhew is surprised to find that 'Sal', is reasonably well-educated and uses words "which few in her position would know how to employ". From an account, perhaps too colourful to be true, Mayhew learns that this Gloucestershire curate's daughter traces her troubles to her decision to take up a governess's post in London. At the time, we hear, she was very pretty and had many admirers, including her employer's only son, who seduces her.

Sal was once dangerously naive, a quality which landed her in trouble more than once. "He promised to marry me", Sal says. "He had a mock-ceremony performed by his footman and I went into lodgings he had taken for me in Gower Street, Tottenham Court Road". For the next six months, they lived together as man and wife. He takes her to the seaside and then abroad, to the spa town of Baden, where they learn of the death of the young man's father, who, because of his son's recent behaviour, has left the young man just enough to purchase a commission in the army. When he hears this, he is "transported with rage." The same evening, he goes to the gaming tables and loses everything. The next morning, he is found in a secluded part of town, having "blown his brains out with a pistol".

Roused to action by the predicament she finds herself in, Sal sells the best part of her wardrobe to pay the bills, planning to return to England. But before she can leave Baden, she meets the man who will complete her ruin, a predatory young officer "of considerable personal attractions". He invites Sal to live with him, making the prospect "so glittering and fascinating that I yielded". The officer explains to the gullible Sal that he would marry her on the spot but if he did, he would forfeit a large sum of money that he is set to inherit in a few years. It "would be folly not to wait until then", he assures her. Sal and her new "paramour" co-habit in London until the officer's leave of absence expires and he returns to Limerick, where his regiment is quartered. Within a fortnight, Sal receives a letter informing her that – for reasons that he is not at liberty to reveal to her – they must separate. He encloses a £50 cheque for her trouble.

When the money is gone, Sal – now ruined, characterless and almost unemployable – is driven to prostitution. For ten years, she lives with one man, then another "until at last I was infected with a disease". She had no idea, she says, of the consequences of neglecting its treatment. "It attacked my face and ruined my features to such an extent that I am hideous to look upon". She tells Mayhew that the prostitutes who congregate nightly on the Haymarket would drive her away "with curses and execrations". Sal's life is now one of desperation and despair. She pays two shillings a week for a room in Perkins' Rents, a slum area of Westminster, and is afraid of being left alone with her thoughts. She has considered converting to Roman Catholicism and getting herself admitted into a convent but is afraid that she has "gone too far to be forgiven". She doesn't think she will live long, anyway, having "some internal disease" that a hospital surgeon has told her will kill her in time. She spends her occasional windfalls on drink and oblivion.

Prostitution is often a way for women to feed alcoholic cravings. Various of Mayhew's informants, including one called Lushing Loo, spend their earnings in beer shops and gin palaces, returning to the streets when the money is gone. Another tragic case is that of a young woman called China Emma, who is "well known to the police...on account of having attempted to drown herself three times". Mayhew describes her as being "short in stature, rather stout" with a blonde complexion and an expressionless face. "There was a look almost of vacuity about her," Mayhew says, with a clinical detachment, "but her replies to my questions were lucid, and denoted that she was only naturally slow and stupid".

Emma tells Mayhew that her parents "kept a grocer's shop in Goswell Street". After her mother dies, Emma's father "took to drinking". In three years, she says, he lost his shop "and in a while killed himself". Alone in the world, Emma meets a sailor "who was very good to me". She becomes one of the "sailors' women", girls kept by sailors while they are ashore. These women, who very often live among the river traffic of the Ratcliffe Highway, may be faithful to their sailors for the duration, but Mayhew still categorises them as species of prostitutes.

After Emma's sailor dies of yellow fever in the West Indies, she meets "a Chinaman called Appoo". Emma says that though he's presently abroad, he "often sends her the needful…I got two pounds from him only the other day". But Emma, like her father, is drinking heavily and no doubt blows whatever cash she has on booze. "Appoo used to treat me badly when I got drunk", she says. "I always get drunk when I've a chance to. Appoo used to tie my legs and arms and take me into the street. He'd throw me into the gutter and then he'd throw buckets of water over me till I was wet through. But that didn't cure it. I don't believe anything would. I'd die for the drink. I must have it and I don't care what I does to get it".

Emma's alcoholism brings on "melancholy fits" when, she says, "I wish I was dead and I run to the water and throw myself in" but, she says ruefully, "I'm always picked out. Once I jumped off a first floor window in Jamaica Place, into the river, but a boatman coming by hooked me up and the magistrate gave me a month".

Lushing in the Gin Palace

If much of the petty crime committed today is fuelled by cheap alcohol, then the middle years of the nineteenth century are no different. Although gin has cleaned up its act since William Hogarth pictured Londoners ruined by the drink a century before, it remains a popular stimulant and the root cause of many social evils.

What makes it more attractive still is the appearance in the 1830s of the 'gin palace'. These big, gaudy and well-lit drinking establishments mushroom and flourish, their opulent fittings, etched glasswork and flaring gas jets drawing people in from dark streets and rough neighbourhoods like moths to a flame. They are to be found in all the poorest districts and here, among more honest clientele, you might see 'lushing' prostitutes, pickpockets spending stolen money, burglars plotting their next housebreaking and ticket of leave men back from the penal colonies. These mingle with ordinary working-class men and women, sometimes with their children, who want only to sit somewhere bright and warm and let a glass of gin ease away the troubles of the day.

Charles Dickens watches the gin shops as they follow trends set by other shops of the day, who are refitting old premises in a bright, modern and opulent style and writes about it in one of his early *Sketches by Boz*. He describes this mania of rebuilding as 'knocking down all the old public houses and depositing splendid mansions, stone balustrades, rosewood fittings, immense lamps and illuminated clocks at the corner of every street'. Dickens says that places of this description 'are inevitably numerous and splendid in precise proportion to the dirt and poverty of the surrounding neighbourhood. The gin shops in and near Drury Lane, Holborn, St Giles, Covent Garden and Clare Market are the handsomest in London'.

Dickens visits Drury Lane, which isn't at its best just then. 'The filthy and miserable appearance of this part of London can hardly be imagined', he says. Walking through the district, Dickens paints a depressing picture of houses with broken windows patched with rags and paper, tenements crammed with families with hungry children and loungers in the street, who smoke, fight and squabble. And then he turns a corner and, he says, 'what a change! All is light and brilliancy'. The gin shop, he says, is a 'gay building' with a 'fantastically-ornamented parapet', an illuminated clock, plate glass windows surrounded by stucco rosettes and a 'profusion of gas-lights in richly-gilt burners', The effect, he notes, is 'perfectly dazzling when contrasted with the darkness and dirt we have just left.'

There's a hum of voices and entering, he finds a warren of rooms, each with its name etched on its glass. In all of these bars are to be seen enormous vats of gin, each labelled with imaginative names such as 'The Cream of the Valley', 'The Out and Out', 'The No Mistake', 'The Regular Flare Up' or 'The Real Knock-me-down'. Dickens describes an elegantly-carved bar of french-polished mahogany which runs the entire width of the place, and the great casks of spirits, whose contents are being dispensed by 'two showily-dressed damsels with large necklaces'.

Among the habitués the young writer picks out for special mention are the 'ostensible proprietor…a stout, coarse fellow in a fur cap, put on very much on one side to give him a knowing air' and two old washer women buying 'half-quarterns of gin and peppermint' who are 'rather overcome by the head-dresses and haughty demeanour of the young ladies who officiate'. Dickens writes amusingly about the people he sees drowning their sorrows in gin. But it's in the last dregs of the evening that the writer's real reaction to the place and what it's doing to the residents of the area is discernible behind a lively account of a drunken brawl:

It is growing late, and the throng of men, women and children…dwindles down to two or three occasional stragglers – cold, wretched-looking creatures in the last stage of emaciation and disease. The knot of Irish labourers at the lower end of the place, who have been alternately shaking hands with and threatening the life of each other for the last hour become furious in their disputes, and finding it impossible to silence one man…

> *they resort to the expedient of knocking him down and jumping on him afterwards. The man in the fur cap and the pot boy rush out; a scene of riot and confusion ensues; half the Irishmen get shut out and the other half get shut in; the pot boy is knocked among the tubs in no time; the landlord hits everybody and everybody hits the landlord; the barmaids scream; the police come in; the rest is a confused mixture of arms, legs, staves, torn coats, shouting and struggling. Some of the party are borne off to the (police) station house and the remainder slink home to beat their wives for complaining and kick the children for daring to be hungry.*

Between the high life enjoyed by Catherine Walters and the depths of despair endured by Sal and Emma, are many others whose stories are equally remarkable and often poignant. 'Martha' from Lyme Regis is one of the "lowest class of women, who prostitute themselves for a shilling or less". Over 40 and shabbily dressed, Martha has a "disreputable and unprepossessing appearance". Visiting an aunt in London, the 16-year-old Martha is standing in the servants' yard one evening when she is spoken to by a man passing by. He affects to be interested in her and invites her to take a stroll with him. "One night we walked longer than usual," Martha says, "and I pressed him to return". The man has other ideas. Feigning exhaustion, he says he would like to rest a while. By an amazing stroke of luck, a very old friend of his lives close by and they will be able to call there before going home.

They find the door open and, seeing another ajar in the passage, they walk in. Here Martha finds an old lady and several girls "dispersed over different parts of the room". When the old woman introduces the girls as her daughters, they laugh so hard they are ordered out. Not surprisingly, Martha is unsettled and asks the man to call a cab. He presses her to drink something before she goes and Martha, refusing a glass of wine, accepts a cup of coffee. "It made me so sleepy", she recalls, "that I begged to be allowed to sit down on the sofa". Martha is advised to rest while a messenger is sent to her aunt. "Of course", she says, "I was drugged and so heavily that I did not regain consciousness till the next morning. I was horrified to discover that I had been ruined and for some days I was inconsolable and cried like a child to be killed or sent back to my aunt".

Martha isn't the only girl whose induction into the ranks of London's prostitutes is effected by means of rape. The young woman who calls herself Agnes tells a story so remarkably similar that you have to wonder whether Martha's experience is a common one or whether elements of the same story are being repeated. Like Sal's tale, this one might derive from the plot of a purple-prosed novel, a romantic play or even a ballad. Mayhew sometimes paid for information and so ran the risk of hearing what his informants thought he wanted.

Now in the service of a bawd in Oxenden Street, Agnes from Matlock in Derbyshire is another 16-year-old who comes up to London to stay with an aunt. When this aunt is indisposed, Agnes, anxious to see the attractions of the city, takes matters into her own hands and goes out on her own. At first, she is enthralled by the crowds of people, the bright shops and the flaring gas lights. But after wandering in strange streets, she finds herself lost, having strayed into alleyways "ever so much darker and quieter". Again echoing Martha's story, she too finds a door standing ajar. She knocks and receiving no answer, knocks louder. At last, she is admitted. She is invited into a parlour by an old woman, who at first takes her to be "one of Lotty's girls" but then becomes very interested to hear that Agnes is a stranger to London. The old woman, having offered her a glass of gin which Agnes is too frightened to refuse, assures her that she knows her aunt well and insists that Agnes stays the night. They'll go together to see the aunt in the morning, she says.

"When I was undressed and in bed", Agnes says, "she brought me a glass of gin and hot water, which she called a night cap and said would do me good. I soon fell into a sound slumber". The night cap is, of course, drugged and "during my state of insensibility, my ruin was accomplished". Since that time, Agnes – perhaps knowing no other option for a fallen woman – has become "this woman's slave". The woman has a house in St James and another in Portland Place and as a prostitute new on the scene, she is "shifted from one to the other". She says that when she is known to the habitues of St James, she is "sent as something new to Portland Place, and so on".

To combat such menaces, well-intentioned do-gooders are getting up committees and lobbying the powers that be about the problem of prostitution on the streets of London. According to Mayhew's figures, there are 'upwards of fifty metropolitan institutions for the reception of the destitute and the reformation of the criminal or those who are exposed to temptation, capable of accommodating collectively about 4,000 persons of both sexes'. The staff of a female mission for 'the rescue of the fallen' distribute tracts to prostitutes and talk with them in streets. They bother them 'in their houses, in the hospitals or in the workhouses' too. Also sounding more like a lot of well-meaning busybodies than an agency of support and help is The East London Association. Composed both of lay and clergy, the association ambitiously aims to check 'that class of public offences which consists in acts of indecency, profaneness, drunkenness and prostitution'. Good luck with that, some must have thought.

But there are other bodies which seem to offer something like real assistance to women who can find no way out of their downward spiral of depravation. The oldest of these is The Magdalen Hospital. Since it was established in 1758, this institution has admitted nearly 9,000 women and it is claimed that about two thirds of these 'have been restored to friends and relations'. Founded in 1835, the London City Mission funds a staff of 389 missionaries and by 1861 has apparently reclaimed 1,230 drunkards, 681 'fallen females' and helped 361 unmarried couples to wed.

Some institutions go further. The Female Aid Society provides training and is open to women who 'from circumstances of poverty, orphanage or sinful conduct in those who should preserve them from evil, are exposed to great temptations' and also welcomes women who are 'weary of sin' and 'desirous of leaving a life of awful depravity and misery'. Meanwhile, other organisations lobby for changes in the law. From 1844, the Associate Institution seeks to improve and enforce the laws for the protection of women. Their crusades against brothels have resulted in up to 300 prosecutions of 'those who have committed criminal assaults upon women and children or who have decoyed them away for immoral purposes'.

But none of this does much good – not really. On the pavements of the Haymarket, where diners are turning out of cafes and supper rooms and the theatres are emptying, the crowds of women in tawdry fashions or dressed like servants in their Sunday best, continue to importune, solicit, amuse and annoy the passers by. Men who might be called 'sporting' or 'of the turf' are attracted like flies and those that don't engage a girl immediately, further obstruct the street as they lounge there smoking cigars and showing off their checkered trousers.

A man who does find a girl to take his fancy and suit his pocket may decide to entertain her at a cafe or take her to one of the gaudy gin palaces to be found up any side street and especially in areas like nearby Covent Garden and Seven Dials. He may though, dispense with all preliminaries and go directly to a house of assignation, where a room and a bed can be had for a couple of shillings.

Introducing houses: meeting a 'woman of the town'

When discretion is required, a gentleman may avail himself of the services of the procuress of an 'introducing house'. Often owned by this figure, these houses 'take in women to board and lodge', Mayhew says, 'but they are quite independent'. To be accepted by the house, the girls 'must be well-known about town'. Henry Mayhew gives an example of how the system works:

'A well-known professional man, a wealthy merchant, an MP, or a rich landed proprietor, calls upon a lady of a house, orders some champagne, and enters into conversation about indifferent matters until he is delicately able to broach the object he had in view. He explains that he wishes to meet with a quiet lady whose secrecy he can rely on and whom he can trust in every possible way'. Needless to say, the lady of the house knows just such a person and promises to do her best to effect an introduction, though she warns the man that the lady may not be at home just now and he may have to wait a little time while she is found.

The girl herself, Mayhew says, 'in all probability does not reside at any great distance', very possibly in areas of Pimlico 'inhabited by beauty that ridicules decorum and laughs at virtuous restrictions.' While he is waiting for the girl to arrive, the customer is plied with champagne, 'every bottle of which costs the consumer fifteen shillings, making a profit to the vendor of at least seventy five per cent. When the lady arrives, the introduction takes place and the matter is finally arranged as far as the introducer is concerned. The woman so-introduced generally gives half the money she obtains from the man to the keeper of the house for the introduction'.

Not everyone goes to Regent Street or the Haymarket to find a girl. A man can find girls in any of the gin palaces and low lodging houses, which operate as *ad hoc* brothels in the East End, and even in pockets of more salubrious areas. Alternatively, he can make himself known to *dollymops*, the maids and servants on errands who have discovered that an afternoon with a gentleman is a quick route to a new bonnet. If he is flush, he can go to supper rooms like Kate Hamilton's, where, until recently, only prosperous men in dinner suits could gain admittance. Kate is a larger-than-life figure in all respects, and holds court from her chair while gentlemen pay well over the odds for her champagne and an introduction to a girl.

But if neither the streets nor the supper rooms suit, a man in need of stimulation might consult one of a number of guide books available to those who know where to look. In the eighteenth century, *Harris's*

List of Covent Garden Ladies, a directory detailing the appearance and specialities of up to 200 prostitutes working in the Covent Garden area, was a publishing sensation. A century later, similarly helpful texts like *The Swell's Night Guide* describe the delights on offer at London's many brothels. If flagellation appeals, he'll find himself catered for at an innocuous address in St John's Wood. If he prefers a young girl or even a virgin, he'll be pointed in the right direction for that, too.

These guides are sometimes disguised as high-minded warnings to the innocent, a ploy I couldn't resist borrowing, when I was writing a Victorian-set novel called *The Edge of the Crowd*:

> ### A Warning to Young Gentlemen and Young Ladies Who Are in Town to Visit The Great Exhibition.
> #### Harold Rutter, B.A. M.A. Phil (Oxon)
> *It is our earnest hope that nothing dangerous or untoward will befall these tourists and that their stay in London will be both happy and profitable. The city offers many diversions of a wholesome nature, but it is regrettably also true that London harbours a multitude of deadlier amusements. That innocent visitors may be cognisant of precisely where dangers lurk, we warn them against the following named places.*
>
> *The Haymarket and Regents Street.*
> *There is no more dreadful sight in all London than that of the scores of painted harlots gathered in The Haymarket and in Regents Street. These pitiable Jezebels ply their awful trade from three in the afternoon until long after midnight has struck and it is hardly possible to traverse the length of either thoroughfare without being made the unwilling subject of numerous propositions of a grossly indecent nature.*
>
> *This area, inclusive of Covent Garden, is alas, not the only place infested by strumpets. Cremorne Gardens from late afternoon is transformed from a place of harmless*

pleasure to a fearsome den of vice. Night houses on Regents Street and Great Windmill Street are only facades, places where prostitutes may be encountered with comparative discretion. The London parks at night are habituated by the most loathsome of creatures, Magdalens too marked by disease to show their faces in God's good daylight.

Despite the best efforts of the Vice Society and humbler crusaders such as ourselves, brothels abound in all areas on the town. Gird well your loins, young passengers, and you shall never find yourself enticed to such dens of terrible iniquity as, for instance, the establishment run by Mrs Newsome, in Curzon Street, wherein are said to be courtesans skilled in the arts of Aphrodite who cater to the most depraved of tastes. Beware too, of a certain address in Circus Road, St John's Wood, which is the notorious haunt of flagellants.

Wych Street and Holywell Street, just North of the Strand.

Here, in shop after shop, are sold what I believe are called "warm gems", species of print and literature that will offend and outrage all but the most corrupt of sensibilities. I am told stereoscopic slides of an unmistakable nature may be purchased now at prices that are dangerously within the compass of a student's pocket.

Be not alarmed: most sojourns in the Great Wen are safe and blameless. Remember too that the church, as ever, offers its sanctuary. In particular, I might mention that young men and vulnerable lady travellers will find safety and solace and good guidance with my little congregation, which gathers at the Reform Chapel, Berners Street, on weekday evenings at 6pm.

This sort of publication is sold alongside a cornucopia of similarly doubtful artefacts in the notorious print shops of Holywell Street. Now demolished to make way for the Aldwych and Kingsway, this 'dingy old Elizabethan thoroughfare' is a place to sidestep if you have the smallest claims to respectability. It's known for its numerous book and print shops, whose windows (where etchings of semi-clad dancing girls compete for space with 'instructive' books and pamphlets), attract the kind of notice that neighbouring second-hand clothes dealers and more reputable booksellers must envy. When the diarist R.D. Blumenfeld visits, he finds these windows 'besieged by a crowd of clerks in their mid-day rest hour'. But perhaps he elbows his way to the front all the same, because he's able to describe the windows and shelves as being 'packed with vicious and gaudy literature, and other material, whose sort is hardly to be matched in the lowest quarters of Paris'.

Costermongers are fond of such lurid literature, Henry Mayhew notes, and copies out an extraordinary example of the purple prose typical of the publications displayed on Holywell Street:

> *With glowing cheeks, flashing eyes and palpitating bosom, Venetia Trelawney rushed back into the refreshment room, where she threw herself into one of the armchairs already noticed. But scarcely had she thus sunk down upon the flocculent cushion when a sharp click, as of some mechanism giving way, met her ears; and at the same instant her wrists were caught in manacles which sprang out of the arms of the treacherous chair, while two steel bands started from the richly carved back and grasped her shoulders. A shriek burst from her lips – she struggled violently, but all to no purpose: for she was a captive – and powerless! We should observe that the manacles and the steel bands which has thus fastened upon her, were covered with velvet, so that they inflicted no positive injury upon her, nor even produced the slightest abrasion of her fair and polished skin.*

This 'narrow, dirty lane' is the epicentre of the Victorian pornography industry. Catharine Arnold, writing in *City of Sin, London and its Vices*

(2010), claims that in 1834, there are '57 pornography shops in this one street, all with a display designed to attract the attention of passers-by'. The display is likely to include 'pornographic novels, erotic prints, etchings and catalogues for prostitutes'. *Fifty seven* porn shops one one short, narrow thoroughfare. No wonder that Holywell Street, like Soho in the late twentieth century, attracts moral indignation and apoplectic letters to the press.

One such letter, written in strangulated tones and fired off to *The Times* in 1849, follows a police raid on the street:

> *Sir, I was much gratified by seeing an account in the police report of* The Times *of this morning of the suppression of at least one of the many shops which now exist in the metropolis for the sale of obscene works and pictures. How is it that so many more are left unmolested has long been a matter of wonder to me. I would direct your attention more especially to Holywell-street and Wych-street, in which are shops the windows of which display books and pictures of the most disgusting and obscene character, and which are alike loathsome to the eye and offensive to the morals of any person of well-regulated mind.*
>
> *'The mischief, however, does not exist merely in the outward display alone – that is perhaps the least part of the danger; but, alas! that is nothing to the effect which such works are calculated to produce on the minds of those persons whose morbid desires induce them eagerly to peruse them, oftentimes to the destruction of their health, and, what is infinitely worse, to their souls' danger.*

The sale of porn in shops or from street barrows draws flak from the moralists, but little is said about the practises of the middle and upper classes, whose appreciation of the genre is in another league. The real connoisseurs of pornography are not the consumers of naughty confessions, lewd prints and guides to the numerous brothels and haunts of flagellants or homosexuals, but sturdy pillars of Victorian establishment itself.

Catherine Arnold suggests that what was often being burned on the garden bonfires that often followed the death of a gentleman was his hoard of pornographic prints and writings: the collections of some gentlemen were considerable. In times past, she says, 'erotica was generally restricted to the upper classes and men of the church' and had been 'since the Renaissance'. To a large extent, the reason for this lies in the history of the genre itself. In medieval times, it was only those with Latin skills – the clergy and the educated – who had access to classical erotic texts. Arnold says that 'the first pornography in English became available during the sixteenth century, with English translations of classical texts such as Adlington's 1567 translation of Apuleius's *The Golden Ass'*.

It wasn't until the nineteenth century, though, that pornography boomed. This was partly because printing became cheaper and books more freely available and also partly, as Donald Thomas points out, because a new, reliable postal system made its discreet dissemination a viable proposition. And, of course, new and interesting possibilities had been opened up by the invention of photography, giving birth not only to the 'dirty postcard' but to stereoscopic images, which offered porn in 3D.

Here in the middle of the century, pornography is collected discreetly as 'curiosa' by educated connoisseurs like Edward Spencer Ashbee, a textile trader and book collector who is amassing what will become the largest collection of erotica and/or pornography ever owned by one person. Ashbee is an obsessive collector and indexer of such materials. He's the author of some works of the subject, too, and writes under the *nom de plume* Pisanus Fraxi. When he dies in 1900, Ashbee's collection is bequeathed to the British Museum, which is eager to acquire his fine editions of Cervantes, but not so keen on being landed with an avalanche of smut. In the sexually repressive age of Victoria, Ashbee obscures his clear fascination with his subject matter by adopting the tones of censure and shock about the texts he writes about.

Ashbee's most extraordinary work in this field is very likely an 11-volume publication presumably not included in the bequest to the British Museum, because Ashbee's name heads the list of authors who may be responsible for that most unique production of Victorian erotica, *My Secret Life*. The hero of this epic account of one man's sexual exploits is called 'Walter' and through the course of 40 years, Walter records his sexual escapades with a seemingly never-ending succession of whores, servants and sometimes very young girls.

Sometimes brutal, always frank and still capable of shocking, the number of Walter's conquests – he claims it was 1,200 – leaves open the possibility that this is the product of an overworked imagination. How could an otherwise ordinary man such as Walter achieve such a tally? However, the number of incidences in which complete satisfaction isn't achieved and the apparent honesty with which he describes how much he loathes himself after some of these, suggests that there's at least a foundation of truth to the *Life*. But whether that life has been Edward Spencer Ashbee's is still to be decided.

Prostitution and pornography is big business. Dr Ryan, the man who estimated that over 80,000 prostitutes are operating in London alone, reckons that £8m is spent yearly on prostitution. 'We cannot authenticate his statements', Mayhew says, and at a time when £1 per week is considered a decent wage, you can see why he's cautious. Ryan's total assumes the average annual income of a prostitute to be £100.

It's not only the prostitutes themselves who are cashing in. Allowing £20 as the average expenses to be deducted from annual earnings, the figure of £1,600,000 is arrived at, leaving '£6,400,000 as the income of the keepers of prostitutes...above £1,000 per annum each', which, he concludes, is 'an enormous income for men in such a situation to derive when compared with the resources of many respectable and professional men'. But keepers of prostitutes are far from being the only people who are making money from sharp practises, as we're about to discover...

CHAPTER 3

Sharp Practises
Swindles and scams

S ome financial advice suited to those living in nineteenth century London: keep your wits about you and your money in a safe place, such as the Government-issued three per cent consols. Don't invest in the latest madcap railway or mining scheme, no matter how attractive its promised returns or how highly-respected and well-connected its proposer. Don't accept drinks from friendly strangers and keep in mind that not everyone is what they seem. Don't believe all you read in documents (they may be forged) and test the coins in your pocket (they could be counterfeit).

If it sounds as though everyone has an angle or is up to some dodge or other, well, it can look very much like that at times. Confidence trickery is a very democratic crime practised at all levels of society – even the best people are at it. Some of these big-time swindlers have left their marks on history and are remembered if not by their own names, then by those of characters invented by writers they inspired.

The two best known confidence tricksters to be found in nineteenth century novels are probably Augustus Melmotte, from Anthony Trollope's *The Way We Live Now* (1875) and Mr Merdle from Dickens's *Little Dorrit* (1857). Both novels satirise the willingness of people at that time to invest heavily in schemes on no sounder basis than the reputation of the scheme's proposer. The mysterious Melmotte, a financier with a hazy past, who sets himself up in fashionable Grosvenor Square and convinces high society to invest in a trans-American railway scheme, can do no wrong – or so it seems. But behind the scenes, Melmotte is hyping the share prices without investing himself. The scheme is really a bottomless scam, which eventually falls through, leading to Melmotte's suicide. It's a fate he shares with Mr Merdle, Dickens's powerful banker, who is able to create a similarly dangerous level of confidence in himself and his grand financial projects:

> *Mr Merdle was immensely rich; a man of prodigious enterprise; a Midas...who turned all he touched to gold. He was in everything good, from banking to building. He was in Parliament, of course. He was in the City, necessarily. He was Chairman of this, Trustee of that, President of the other. The weightiest of men had said to projectors, "Now, what name have you got? Have you got Merdle?" And, the reply being in the negative, had said, "Then I won't look at you".*

But, like Melmotte's railway, Merdle's is a hollow business and when it implodes, Merdle goes with it. In both cases, people queue up to invest in schemes run by men whose outward shows of wealth and position have convinced them that the scheme will not only be safe but highly profitable. Either of these fictional characters might have been based on the real Irish MP, John Sadleir, who kills himself after the collapse of the Tipperary Bank threatens to reveal his dodgy speculations in rail and mining companies.

Sadleir's case is far from being a lone instance. The role model for Becky Sharp, Thackeray's artful protagonist in *Vanity Fair* (1843), is the equally interesting Eliza Frances Robertson, known as 'the Blackheath Swindler'. At the turn of the century, Robinson manages to build herself a life of luxury and connection based entirely on people's willingness to believe that she has recently come into a fortune, which will be available as soon as an estate is settled.

Trust is the mainstay of any confidence trick, but adopting a dog collar can instantly establish your place in society, too. Mayhew tells of a man calling himself the Rev Mr Williams who, 'by means of forged credentials…obtained an appointment as curate in Northamptonshire, where he conducted himself for some time with a most sanctimonious air. Several marriages were celebrated by him'. Later, this self-made man of the cloth manages to obtain 'many articles of jewellery from firms in London, who were deceived by his appearance and position'. A more common ploy is for people of fashionable or respectable appearance to pretend they are to be married and 'wish to have their house furnished'. Mayhew offers an example:

> *A case of this kind occurred in Grove Terrace where a furniture dealer was requested to call on a swindler by a person who pretended to be his servant and received instructions to send him various articles of furniture. The goods were accordingly sent to the house. On a subsequent day the servant called on him at his premises, with a well-dressed young lady whom she introduced as the intended wife of her employer and said they had called to select some more goods. They selected a variety of articles and desired they should be added to the account. One day the tradesman called for payment and was told the gentleman was then out of town but would call on him as soon as he returned. Soon after, he made another call at the house, which he found closed up and that he had been heartlessly duped. The value of the goods amounted to £58 18s 4d.*

A woman calling herself Mrs Major Gordon, who claimed her husband was in India, 'succeeded in obtaining goods from different tradesmen…to a great amount'. Mayhew says that 'possessing a ladylike appearance and address, she easily succeeded in obtaining a furnished residence in St John's Wood and applied to a livery stable keeper for the loan of a brougham, hired a coachman and got a suit of livery for him and appeared in West End assemblies as a lady of fashion. After staying about a fortnight in St John's Wood she left suddenly, without settling with any of her creditors. She was convicted at Marylebone police court under the name of Mrs Helen Murray, charged with obtaining goods by fraudulent means'.

Some Victorian swindles are still practised today. In the mid-nineteenth century, advertisements appear in newspapers promising to find situations for working men, servants, clerks, teachers, clergymen and others. The swindler behind these ads, who often will have rented an empty house as a dead letter drop, charges an agent's fee to the employer and to the prospective employee, pocketing both. Mayhew reports one such case where the house is watched and a women seen to take the letters away. On arresting the woman, the police officers, he says:

> *found in her basket 80 letters, 44 of them containing 5s in postage stamps or a postal order made payable to the swindler himself. Nearly all the others were letters from persons…who promised to send the money when they got an opportunity. On a subsequent day, 120 letters were taken out of the letter box, most of them containing a remittance. The system had been in operation for a month. One day, 190 letters were delivered by one post. It was estimated that no fewer than 3000 letters had come in during the month, most of them enclosing 5/- and it is supposed the swindler has received about £700, a handsome return for the price of a few advertisements in newspapers, a few lithographed circulars, a few postage stamps and a quarter of a year's rent of an empty house.*

For a scam to succeed, the scammer must have *chutzpah*, the sort of audacious gall which convinces people that what he says is the God's honest truth. The Cacique (or Prince) of Poyais, a small South American kingdom, has this very quality in spades. George MacGregor, as the Prince was born in 1786, has been a soldier and adventurer before he dubs himself Cacique of an imaginary country he calls Poyais and invites British and French investors to speculate on the untapped reserves of gold and silver in his fictional kingdom.

MacGregor is used to awarding himself elevated titles. His rank of Colonel is an unearned promotion and 'Sir' George MacGregor's knighthood is equally fictitious.

After serving in the British army and fighting in the Peninsular war, MacGregor sails to South America, where he has further adventures in the Venezuelan army. Not everyone sees him as the upstanding British soldier he pretends to be. "I am sick and tired of this bluffer, or Quixote, or the devil knows what", writes one official. "This man can hardly serve us... without heaping ten thousand embarrassments upon us".

 MacGregor returns to London in 1820 as the self-styled Cacique of Poyais, and is so convincing that he and his South American wife are accepted and courted by society as the rulers of a strangely Anglophile kingdom whose natives are friendly and whose natural resources need only the oil of investment to spring from the ground. Money is being invested in all sorts of South American projects at this time and MacGregor's scheme sounds more attractive and a safer bet than many. People clamour to buy bonds and rights. The price per acre of land quickly rises from 3s 3d to 4s, enabling MacGregor to borrow heavily against the future wealth of his kingdom. Everyone wants a piece of the action.

For some, the lure of this magical kingdom is sufficient for them to sell up and become one of the 70 would-be settlers who board the *Honduras Packet,* which sails from London in September 1822, bound for Poyais. In January of the following year, another 200 leave Scotland on the *Kennersley Castle.* What happens next must have given Charles Dickens plenty of inspiration for the American land swindle in *Martin Chuzzlewit,* as well as the dealings of corrupt financier Merdle in *Little Dorrit.*

Rather than the lush fertile land promised, the settlers find only dense, uninhabitable jungle and the ruins of a failed attempt at settlement made in the previous century. The ships that brought them to this inhospitable coast have left for England long before the settlers discover the true extent of their plight. While some build rudimentary shelters, others despair and at least one man commits suicide. It is only by enormous good fortune that the settlers are discovered only a few weeks later by the crew of a passing ship. By his time, they are in a very sorry state. Hunger and disease have taken a dreadful toll. Many are dead, and more will die on the voyage home. In all, only 60 of the 240 settlers who arrived on the coast of what is now the Gulf of Honduras, (also known as the Mosquito Coast) survive their terrible ordeal.

The Poyais fiasco has ended in tragedy on a huge scale but perhaps for George MacGregor, it's only an annoying setback. He avoids the repercussions of his crime by decamping from England and actually has the nerve to try his Poyais scheme again – and with some success – in France. MacGregor continues to mount scams based on his mythical Poyais, or similarly doubtful places in Polynesia, for the rest of his life. This tenacious nuisance is still attempting to sell pieces of Poyais in 1837, seven years before his death in Caracas, Venezuela, where he has gone to claim an army pension.

Swindles are carried on 'very extensively in the metropolis in different classes of society'. Lodgers rent rooms and do moonlight flits before the next instalment is due; diners leave unpaid restaurant bills, thimble and pea men dupe passers-by on street corners and mock auctions attract those willing to believe that all that glitters is indeed gold. Cheques are forged, wills are altered, money is counterfeited and embezzled by 'commercial travellers, clerks in lawyers' offices, banks, firms and government offices'.

People established in apparently respectable trades may have lucrative sidelines. Henry Mayhew talks to a photographer who took to the business after deciding that he might "like it better" than busking with his banjo. He knows nothing about photography, or taking the portraits he hopes will give him a living. His first attempt is not a success, of course. "I didn't know how to make the portrait and it was all black when I took the glass out", he says. With amazing cheek, the photographer tells his customer "that it would come out bright as it dried and he went away quite delighted".

His next efforts aren't much better, but such is the general ignorance of this new invention, that "everybody was quite pleased with their spotted and black pictures". The photographer and his assistant Jim have their own portraits taken by other, more accomplished photographers and these they exhibit as their own work. The photographer's skill improves markedly after he refers to "the sixpenny book of instructions" and by lowering his prices and working on Sundays, the pair are soon doing a brisk trade.

Despite this, he says, "we are obliged to to resort to all sorts of dodges to make sixpenny portraits pay....one of our dodges is what we term 'an American air-preserver", which is nothing more than a card or...even brown paper". Once a customer has sat for a sixpenny or a shilling portrait, the photographer shows him an 'air-preserver' and tells him that without one of these, his picture will fade. "I also tell them that I make nothing out of them...and that makes 'em buy one directly", he tells Mayhew. "We've actually had people come to us to have our preservers put upon other persons' portraits, saying they've been everywhere for them and can't get them". He adds that they have "actually had photographers themselves come in to buy our American air-preservers".

Mayhew's photographer seems to spend more time dreaming up cons than taking photographs. "Another dodge", the man says, "is I always take the portrait on a shilling size and after they are done, I show them what they can have for a shilling – the full size, with the knees and table and vase on it – and let them understand that for sixpence they have all the background and legs cut off".

If the photograph fails to process properly, the photographer's assistant "wraps it in a large piece of paper so that it will take some time to unroll it, at the same time crying out, 'take sixpence from the lady, if you please'". If the image is discovered to be a dud, the customer is told that it "will become better as it dries and come to your natural complexion". Should this customer remain unsatisfied – or even become suspicious – the photographer will offer to have the photograph "passed through the brightening solution" after which it "will come out lighter in an hour or two". The photograph is immersed in water, dried off and wrapped up, the customer being told not to expose it to air for a couple of hours. If he returns to complain, "we take another portrait and charge them 3d more".

Incredibly, some people are happy to accept photographs of other people as being good likenesses of themselves. If people are in a hurry, rather than lose a sale while the image is developed, the photographer will present his sitter with one of the many samples from his window. "One day a young lady came in and wouldn't wait, so Jim takes a specimen from the window and, as luck would have it, it was a portrait of a widow in her cap". Unluckily for him, the woman insists on opening her package before she leaves the premises, and complains. "This isn't me", she says, "it's got a widow's cap and I was never married in my life!" Jim insists that the photograph is a correct likeness ("and so it was, but it wasn't of her") and convinces the young woman that the widow's cap is only a shadow cast by her hair and she "took it away believing that such was the case".

"The fact is, people don't know their own faces", the photographer says, "Half of 'em have never looked in a glass half a dozen times in their life and directly they see a pair of eyes and a nose, they fancy they are their own". But when Jim tries to fob off another subject with a photograph from the window, she objects strongly, mainly to the child who is included in the composition. "Jim looked at her, and then at the picture, as if comparing and, says he, 'it certainly is a wonderful likeness, miss, and one of the best we ever took. It's the way you sat; and what has occasioned it was a child passing through the yard'. She supposed it was so and took the portrait away highly delighted".

And then there is the occasion when the con is taken too far. When an old woman needs her photograph immediately, she is presented with their last remaining specimen. It's a very dark photograph, but when the woman puts on her spectacles, she's able to discern the image of a sailor. "I ain't a man", she objects, and the photographer has to admit that this time at least, they may have been "a little too strong".

Such is the fascination with photography that the public will believe whatever they are told. "People think the camera will do anything", the photographer tells Mayhew. For a extra 2d, customers can be 'mesmerised' by the camera. They are made to stare at the camera for two or three minutes…until their eyes water". What benefit they are supposed to derive from this isn't explained. Another dodge employed regularly is rather more dangerous. "I also profess to remove warts", the photographer admits, "by touching them with nitric acid. My price is a penny a wart, or a shilling for the job…my wart patients seldom come twice, for they screams out ten thousand blue murders when the acid bites them".

Park Life: pickpockets and prostitutes

Criminals find easy pickings wherever people congregate. Railway termini, where people are distracted by the business of catching and disembarking from trains are ideal places for pickpockets and drag thieves. The crowds offer a choice of pockets, the chance for concealment and the opportunity for the thief to lose himself once the theft is accomplished.

Crowded omnibuses and river piers where people wait for steam boats are profitable haunts for dippers, as are the new department stores and the bustling pubs and gin palaces. Public processions and parades, race meetings, grand openings and any event promising to draw crowds is also guaranteed to draw the criminal element. Although the crime rate at the Great Exhibition of 1851 is surprisingly low, this is attributed to a much larger than usual police presence.

Venues offering a variety of interesting possibilities to the criminally-minded of the early to mid-century are London's pleasure gardens. At Vauxhall on the South Bank, and Ranelagh and Cremorne (situated at opposite ends of Chelsea) prostitutes scan the strolling crowds for likely customers, while the job of the pickpocket is made easier by pleasure seekers engrossed by the musical bands, fireworks, hot air balloon ascents, noisy swells in the restaurant booths, tightrope walkers – or by distractions of a more romantic kind. The shady walks of the gardens where the light from as many as 15,000 tree-hung lanterns doesn't penetrate, have long proven ideal for assignations.

The oldest of these London landmarks is Vauxhall, which was doing business as New Spring Gardens as early as 1660. After enjoying their heydays in the eighteenth century, by the middle of the nineteenth they are losing their gloss. Although the clientele is mostly well-dressed and behaves with decorum, there are also parties of young bucks out on the spree and enough punch-sozzled visitors to offer easy pickings for the prostitutes and pickpockets alike.

Like the pickpockets who dress as dandies to disappear into crowds and the prostitutes whose second-hand wear is good enough to allow them in, the parks are a sham, illusions conjured by the night, the lights and the ambience created by music, laughter and alcohol. As early as the 1830s, Dickens had visited Vauxhall by day, and had a very different experience, as he recorded in *Sketches by Boz*:

> *We paid our shilling at the gate, and then we saw for the first time, that the entrance, if there had been any magic about it at all, was now decidedly disenchanted, being, in fact, nothing more nor less than a combination of very roughly-painted boards and sawdust. We glanced at the orchestra and supper-room as we hurried past – we just recognised them, and that was all. We bent our steps to the firework-ground; there, at least, we should not be disappointed. We reached it, and stood rooted to the spot with mortification and astonishment. That the Moorish tower – that wooden shed with a door in the centre, and daubs of crimson and yellow all round, like a gigantic watch-case! That the place where night after night we had beheld the undaunted Mr. Blackmore make his terrific ascent, surrounded by flames of fire, and peals of artillery, and where the white garments of Madame Somebody (we forget even her name now), who nobly devoted her life to the manufacture of fireworks, had so often been seen fluttering in the wind, as she called up a red, blue, or party-coloured light to illumine her temple!*

You're likely to encounter swindlers on the streets too, *magsmen* (or *sharpers)* in particular. Magsmen, says Mayhew, are 'a peculiar class of unprincipled men who play tricks with cards, skittles etc and lay wagers with the view of cheating those strangers who may have the misfortune to be in their company'. There are usually three of them in a gang, he says. 'They go out together but do not walk beside each other when they are at work. One may be on one side of the street and the other two arm-in-arm on the other. They generally dress well and in various styles; some are attired as gentlemen, others as country farmers. In one gang, a sharper is dressed as a coachman in livery and in another they have a confederate attired as a parson...wearing green spectacles'. You can see them wandering about the streets till four o'clock in the afternoon.

'The person who walks the street in front of the gang is generally the most engaging and social; the other two keep in sight and watch his movements...If he sees a countryman or foreigner who appears to have money, or a person loitering by a shop window...he enters into conversation about some object in sight. For instance, in passing Somerset House in the Strand, he will...ask what noble building that is, hinting at the same time that he is a stranger in London'. His first object is 'to learn from the person the locality to which he belongs. The sharp informs him he has some relation there or knows a person in the town or district'. He will make out that he has money and may claim, as in the following instance, that he is going back there to give some of his wealth to the poor.

'It sometimes happens that...he proposes to give the stranger a sum of money to distribute to the poor of his district, as he is specially interested in them and may at the same time produce his pocket-book with a bundle of flash notes'. Now that the dupe is confident that his new friend is not after his cash, he may agree to his invitation to take a drink with him at 'a beer shop or gin palace to have a glass of ale or wine'. They will then go on to another public house which has a skittles alley. Friendly bets are laid and the victim is allowed to win his first game before, of course, being thoroughly fleeced.

Even beggars are often not what they seem. Mayhew, naturally, carefully catalogues the range of dubious mendicants to be encountered on London streets. Among those wheedling cash under false pretences are, he observes, 'turnpike sailors' (beggars who dress and talk like seamen but whose only nautical experience may have been crossing the river on a ferryboat), beggars feigning all kinds of injuries and disabilities and those who claim to be the victims of the latest industrial or economic disasters. Some, he says, bind their legs to produce a puffy, inflamed appearance while others apply certain products to counterfeit festering wounds.

More intriguing are the begging-letter writers, whose letters are as skilfully worded as today's junk mail scams and who adopt practised personas when meeting their victims in person. Very often they appear as shabby genteel, educated men who have fallen on hard times through no fault of their own. Mayhew's portrait of one importuner also offers a good idea of his own observational skills. The man he talks to:

> *affects white cravats, soft hands and filbert nails. He oils his hair, cleans his boots and wears a portentous stick-up collar. The light of other days of gentility and comfort casts a halo of deportment over his well-brushed, white-seamed coat, his carefully darned blackcloth gloves and pudgy gaiters. He invariably carries an umbrella and wears a hat with an enormous brim. His once-raven hair is turning grey and his well-shaved and whiskerless cheeks are blue as with gunpowder tattoo. He uses the plainest and most respectable of cotton pocket-handkerchiefs and keeps his references as to character in the most irreproachable of shabby leather pocket books. His mouth is heavy, his underlip thick, sensual and lowering and his general expression of pious resignation contradicted by restless, bloodshot eyes that flash from side to side, quick to perceive the approach of a compassionate looking clergyman or female devotee, or a keen-scented member of the Society for the Suppression of Mendicity.*

Commonly, the begging letter writer will pretend to be a decayed gentleman who claims some tenuous link with the family he's applying to for some 'trifling assistance'. He will offer convincing testimonials and perhaps say, with a sigh, that his money has become tied up in the courts of Chancery. Posing as an educated scholar, he will explain that he is unable to take up an usher's post at a distant school, as he can't raise the train fare. In the guise of a literary man, he may bring out dog-eared copies of verse and beg for patronage. The begging letter writer may appear in different guises to different people and to be successful, he must, of course, remember exactly to whom he has told what. Some beggars are known to keep notebooks or *registers* for just this purpose.

'It would not do to tell the same story twice', Mayhew advises, 'as once happened to an unusually audacious member of the fraternity, who had obtained money from an old lady for the purpose of burying his wife'. Confident in the old lady's kindness of heart and weakness of memory, he appears again at the old lady's door only three months later, again in a state of high emotion. He tells her that the 'wife of his bosom, the mother of his children, had left him for that bourn from which no traveller returns' and that 'owing to a series of unprecedented and unexpected misfortunes, he had not sufficient money to defray the funeral expenses' – and is promptly interrupted by his intended victim.

"Nonsense!" she says. "You lost your wife a quarter of a year ago. You couldn't have lost her twice, and as to marrying again and losing again in that short time, it is quite impossible!"

CHAPTER 4

Murder and Mayhem
Panic on the streets of Victorian London

In September, 1850, a gentleman on his way home cuts through Regent's Park at midnight and is joined by two young men heading in the same direction. The gent is making small talk – perhaps he is tipsy or nervous about his unexpected company – when the men attack him. His mouth is covered with a wad of material and his head is gripped in an armlock while the men rifle his pockets. He struggles but is immediately knocked down by a blow from behind (a cosh or 'life-preserver' he thinks). As he comes to, he hears the footsteps of his assailants receding as they run off.

He has been chloroformed and it's a few moments before he can think straight and call out "Murder!" Police arrive in about three minutes. One of the constables says that he met the attackers near the toll-gate but mistook them for drunken gents larking about. The victim (who wrote to *The Times* about his ordeal) was probably himself drunk. Would you take a shortcut through a park at midnight?

A letter to the same newspaper the following year complains that *highway robbery with violence to the person* is alarmingly common and unlikely to be detected. This correspondent's experience is similar. He too is returning home when, without warning, finds himself 'suddenly seized from behind by someone who, placing the bend of his arm to my throat and then clasping his right wrist with his left hand' forms a 'powerful lever'. Partially strangled, the man is unable to call for help although, he says, 'there was plenty at hand'. While this is happening, a second assailant searches his pockets. He is then 'thrown violently to the ground' where he is left to come to his senses. The attack occurs on 'one of the most frequented highways out of London' in sight, he says, of two other pedestrians and 'within the hearing and almost within sight of three policemen'.

The victims of these attacks are not alone. Someone at Lincoln's Inn, a lawyer, perhaps, writes – to *The Times*, again – after he too is attacked 'in a public thoroughfare' and suffers 'constriction of the throat', while another talks of being 'struck on the head with a life-preserver'. In all these incidents, the victim is forcibly held by the neck while he is robbed by a second man. 'Garotting' – a term which is coming to denote both this and other variations of what we would call muggings – is reported spasmodically throughout the 1850s but becomes the cause of a brief but widespread panic in 1862, when MP Hugh Pilkington, returning home after a late session in the House, is garotted and robbed of his watch.

The press has a field day. Some papers, *The Times* in particular, see a chance to use this as a hobby horse to call for a tougher stance on crime. Others run lurid and highly imaginative illustrations with their reporting. Fanned by the press, the fear of garotting becomes a general panic and while figures suggest that the response is disproportionate to the reality. The streets of the capital – during the six months that the panic lasts – become places of (mostly imagined) danger.

Henry Mayhew has by now severed his connection with the satirical magazine he co-founded with Mark Lemon in 1841. *Punch*, though, continues to thrive and is in its element in 1862, when the garotte panic peaks and inspires some acerbic editorials and witty cartoons. One illustration depicts a garotter nursing his injured hands while his intended victim – who is sporting a spiked 'anti-garotte collar' – walks on, oblivious to the attack. Another cartoon shows a 'Mr Tremble' wearing a ludicrously wide skirt. According the caption, Mr Tremble has drawn inspiration 'from his wife's crinoline' to invent a 'patent anti-garotte coat' whose hoops spread so widely that it 'places him completely out of harm's reach as he walks home from the city'. The coat is an invention but the spiked collar is really available to anyone who cares more about their absolute safety than their appearance.

Although this scare is exaggerated by both press and rumour mill, and the definition of garotting is in many cases extended to include even pickpockets (thus inflating figures considerably), garotting is a real crime. Citizens are suffering concerted attacks by assailants usually working in pairs, not only in ill-lit and empty streets, but in broad daylight on fairly populous thoroughfares too, if the letters to newspapers are to be believed. That so many attacks are made in the same fashion suggests that rendering the victim incapable by half strangling him has become something of a craze among those predisposed to violent street robbery. If so, then what is the cause?

It has been suggested that at bottom of this sudden surge may be the fact that there are now more convicts on the streets. David Wilson, Professor of Criminology at the University of Central England, suggests that with Australia then accepting fewer and fewer convict transports – the practise of exporting felons to the colony finally ends in 1868 – the function of prisons shifted from holding centres for those sentenced to transportation to places where prisoners served out their sentences. On top of this, more convicts have returned from Australia and Tasmania and the term 'ticket of leave man' already has fearful connotations in the public mind.

In fact, so hard did returning convicts find getting on their feet again that Henry Mayhew heard their grievances at a meeting of ticket of leave men he convened in Holborn in 1856. It seems too convenient to lay the blame for the garoting spree on the ticket-of-leavers, though this song of the time does just that:

THE SONG OF THE GAROTTER

OH, Meet me by moonlight alone,
And then I will give you the hug,
With my arm round your neck tightly thrown,
I'm as up to the work as a Thug.
Behind you I softly will creep,

MURDER AND MAYHEM

And taking you quite unawares,
On my prey like a tiger I'll leap;
If I happen to choke you, who cares?
I'm out with a ticket of leave,
Which by gulling the chaplain I got,
And I'm free to maim, murder and thieve,
For a cove he must live, must he not?
So meet me by moonlight alone,
Kind stranger, I beg and entreat,
And I'll make all your money my own,
And leave you half dead in the street.
(*Punch*, December 27, 1862)

The results of this moral panic must please those arguing for a stiffening up of the justice system. Following the garrotting hysteria, tougher prison regimes are introduced and the recommended sentence for anyone convicted of the crime is now prison and flogging, which is reintroduced in a reaction to the scare. It also results in further constrictions on the movements of the much-maligned ticket of leave men.

And are the streets of Victoria's London more dangerous than today? It depends where you go. Of course, there are streets and districts where you'd be advised to tread carefully or visit, as Mayhew did, in the company of a policeman. What remains of the rookery of St Giles, the streets of Seven Dials, Whitechapel and Spitalfields, the Borough and Bermondsey are all places where you should keep a close grip on your possessions and an eye out for trouble. Be wary too of locations along the river. The Ratcliffe Highway, Wapping and Limehouse, with their transient populations of sailors, smugglers, prostitutes, pickpockets, and the desperately poor, can also be dangerous. The narrow, overcrowded courts and alleys of these settlements can be pressure cookers and disputes are settled with fists. Fights are common – and the participants are by no means exclusively male. Here's Charles Dickens, writing of a visit to a lively part of Seven Dials:

a little crowd has collected round a couple of ladies, who, having imbibed the contents of various 'three-outs' of gin and bitters in the course of the morning, have at length differed on some point of domestic arrangement, and are on the eve of settling the quarrel satisfactorily, by an appeal to blows, greatly to the interest of other ladies who live in the same house, and tenements adjoining, and who are all partisans on one side or other.

"Vy don't you pitch into her, Sarah?" exclaims one half-dressed matron, by way of encouragement. "Vy don't you? if MY 'usband had treated her with a drain last night, unbeknown to me, I'd tear her precious eyes out – a wixen!"

Take care too, if you like a drink. Mayhew identifies a 'very common class of male thieves' who, like our garotters, prey on drunks. 'You occasionally find them loafing in tap-rooms', he says. *Bug-hunters*, as they are called, 'watch for drunken people' and find ways of luring them into 'some court or slum', where they are stripped of their 'watch, money or other valuables'. These are 'loafers and low ruffians', he says, the sort who steal lead from houses and copper boilers from kitchens and wash-houses, and who aren't above committing their robberies 'in the public urinals at a late hour of the night'.

It's not safe to appear vulnerable on the streets and walking unsteadily is a sure way to attract unwanted attention. There is another class of thieves who steal from drunken persons, Mayhew says, especially at dusk. He describes their method:

Two women, respectably dressed, meet a drunken man in the street, stop him and ask him to treat them. They adjourn to the bar of a public house for the purpose of getting some gin or ale. While drinking at the bar, one of the women tries to rob him of his watch or money. A man who is called a stickman, an accomplice and possibly a paramour of hers, comes to the bar a short time after them. He has a glass of some kind of liquor and stands between the two females and this man. If they have by this time secured the booty, it is passed to the latter, who thereupon slips away, with the stolen articles in his possession.

If anything goes awry, the stickman is there to offer the threat of violence.

Of course, sticks aren't the only weapons used on the streets of Victorian London. A knife is easily concealed and its wounds are often lethal, which perhaps is why so many assailants prefer something which will earn them less than a capital sentence, should they be caught. We've seen the cosh or 'life-preserver' resorted to on a number of occasions already. This comes in a variety of guises – a piece of leather filled with sand, a stick with a big, bulbous end or a heavy lead ball on a cord. In Mayhew's experience, robberies perpetrated with such a weapon are 'usually done by one or more brutal men following a woman'.

The woman, he says, 'walks as if she was a common prostitute… She picks up a man in the street, possibly the worse for liquor; she enters into a conversation and decoys him to some quiet, secluded place and may there allow him to take liberties with her person'. While he is distracted in this way, she robs him of his valuables and makes off. In some cases, we're told, her victim will chase after her, which is when one of the men may stop her pursuer with some innocent question, or a request for directions.

Another effective ploy is for one of the men to play the outraged husband and to demand what the dupe has been playing at with his so-called wife, threatening to 'punish him for indecent conduct with her'. During the altercation, the woman will make good her escape. In some cases, though, the victim 'is not only plundered of his money, but severely injured by a life-preserver or bludgeon'.

It's not surprising, then, that some Londoners protect themselves with personal weapons of their own. There is a brisk trade in these, which suggests a nervousness about walking the streets. Some weapons are as ingenious as they are deadly: sword sticks, popular in the eighteenth century, are still regarded as useful accessories in the nineteenth: umbrellas with daggers; walking cane guns, too, (though I've yet to uncover an instance of their use); heavy-headed canes; shillelaghs; wooden truncheons and knuckledusters.

The ability to protect oneself and others is a matter of importance, as Ben Miller points out in his *Out of this Century* blog. He notes that an 1879 publication on deportment insists that 'A man should be able to defend himself from ruffians, if attacked, and also to defend women from their insults', while *Dunbar's Complete Handbook of Etiquette* (1884) advises that the martial arts are ideal improvers of both body and mind:

> *It is a matter of the first importance to the young aspirant that he attend to the training and deportment of his body, as well as that of his mind. Besides, his physical bearing has much to do with that command of address, which is so noted a characteristic of the thoroughbred gentleman. The body should be properly "set" by gymnastics, fencing, dancing, drill, or other physical exercises.*

Miller quotes from the work of an original expert on the subject. The Westminster-educated peer, author, boxer and convert to Islam, Rowland George Allanson-Winn, 5th Baron Headley – who later adopts the name Shaikh Rahmatullah al-Farooq. Allanson-Winn is one of those extraordinary Victorians whose eclectic range of interests borders on the eccentric. Whatever you make of him, you wouldn't want to come across him on a dark and rainy night, not if you've read his treatise *Broadsword and Singlestick*.

This, according to Allanson-Winn, comprises 'a few ideas on the subject of attack and defence with weapons other than those with which nature has endowed us' and offers instruction on the arts of fencing, the correct use of the quarter-staff, broadsword and bayonet, but also a chapter on more readily-available weapons. Having considered the merits of the cudgel, shillelagh, walking-stick (the best wood to have them made from, the most effective weight and so on) and accompanying each section with helpful diagrams illustrating the poses to be adopted when wielding his weapons, Allanson-Winn moves on to consider the use of that most vicious of weapons, the umbrella.

He complains that 'as a weapon of modern warfare this implement has not been given a fair place'. The umbrella has even, he laments, 'been spoken of with contempt and disdain'. This is a great shame, he thinks, because even in the hands of 'a strong and angry old woman' the umbrella can cause a lot of damage. Don't smile – before expertly advising on the use of this weapon, the author offers a word of caution:

> *It is, of course, an extremely risky operation prodding a fellow-creature in the eye with the point of an umbrella and I once knew a man who, being attacked by many roughs, and, in danger of losing his life through their brutality, in a despairing effort made a desperate thrust at the face of one of his assailants. The point entered the eye and the brain, and the man fell stone dead at his feet. I would therefore only advocate the thrusting when extreme danger threatens – as a dernier resort, in fact, and when it is a case of who shall be killed, you or your assailant.*

But, if you can be trusted with something this deadly, then you have a choice of holding it like a fencing foil and making long thrusts from a distance or taking it with both hands, as a soldier grasps his rifle at bayonet practise. This last hold, the author says, makes the umbrella perfect for use against several assailants at close quarters. In this case, he advises, 'the arms should be bent and held close to the body, which should be made to work freely from the hips, so as to put plenty of weight into the short sharp prods with which you can alternately visit your opponents' faces and ribs'.

There's more: 'If you have the handle in your right hand, and the left hand grasps the silk (or alpaca), not more than a foot from the point, it will be found most effective to use the forward and upward strokes with the point for the faces, and the back-thrusts with the handle for the bodies. Whatever you do, let your strokes be made very quickly and forcibly, for when it comes to such close work as this, your danger lies in being altogether overpowered, thrown down, and possibly kicked to death; and, as I have before hinted, when there is a choice of evils, choose the lesser, and don't be the least squeamish about hurting those who will not hesitate to make a football of your devoted head, should it unfortunately be laid low'.

It will take more than an umbrella to defend yourself against some villains, especially ones who appear not to be human. At a quarter to nine on the evening of 20 February 1838, in the village of Old Ford in what is now London's East End, 18-year-old Jane Alsop gets a nasty shock. According to the testimony she gives after the event, Jane hears 'a violent ringing at the gate at the front of the house'. Opening the door, she sees a cloaked figure. The man, who claims to be a police officer, says "For God's sake, bring me a light, for we have caught Springheeled Jack here in the lane".

According to *The Times* of 22 February, Jane has no sooner given the man a lighted candle than he 'threw off his outer garment and applying the lighted candle to his breast, presented a most hideous and frightful appearance, and vomited forth a quantity of blue and white flames from his mouth.' His eyes, adds *The Times*, 'resembled red balls of fire'. Nor is this extraordinary figure's attire any less startling. Jane (daughter of a 'respectable invalid') recalls that he had worn a large helmet and a very close-fitting garment resembling white oilskin.

The Times describes Jane's ordeal:

> *Without uttering a sentence, he darted at her, and catching her partly by her dress and the back part of her neck, placed her head under one of his arms, and commenced tearing her gown with his claws, which she was certain were of some metallic substance. She screamed out as loud as she could for assistance, and by*

considerable exertion got away from him, and ran toward the house to get in. Her assailant, however, followed her and caught her on the steps leading to the half-door, when he again used considerable violence, tore her neck and arms with his claws as well as a quantity of hair from her head.

Jane is at last 'rescued from his grasp by one of her sisters'.

This sister attests to Jane's version of events, convincing at least *The Times* that this isn't the fantasy of a young girl who has read one too many gothic novels. The newspaper no doubt welcomes the account, coming as it does, hot on the heels of other reports of a bizarre creature who has earned himself the sobriquet of 'Springheeled Jack'. 'Jack' made his debut the year before, in the village of Barnes in south west London, appearing there as a 'ghost, imp or devil' or in the shape of a large white bull and committing a number of assaults upon women in the area. You may note a disparity in appearance between the various Jacks in Barnes and the Jack in Old Ford, but no matter, to a credulous public living in unsettled times – and also to newspaper editors hungry for sensation – the attacks have been made by one and the same man. Or a bull, or even a baboon, as is later reported.

Eight days after Jane Alsop is attacked, and within a short walk of her house, Lucy Scales (also 18) and her sister are assaulted by a tall, thin and gentlemanly figure attired in bonnet-like headwear and a cloak. A flash of blue flame leaves Lucy temporarily blinded and subject to 'violent fits'. In this case the attacker, disappears into the night with no further violence. Springheeled Jack – so-called because of his apparent ability to evade capture by making superhuman leaps over walls – is already a sensation in London and its outlying villages. On Commercial Road, a servant boy opens the house door to a man of 'hideous appearance' and screams so loudly that the visitor runs off.

At the White Lion pub in Vere Street, a well-dressed man announces that he is Springheeled Jack and proceeds to attack a woman with a club. In Lincoln's Inn Fields, a woman has her face slapped by a cloaked man – and surely only Springheeled Jack could commit such an outrage. Sightings of Jack are made from Herne Hill to Brighton and according to rumour, Jack so alarms residents of South London boroughs that several die of fright. The daughter of a Plutarch Dickinson is so frightened by a spectral being 'enveloped in a white sheet and blue fire' that, it is reported, she is now 'in a very dangerous state'.

The passing of the years has no effect on Jack's tireless efforts to outrage Victoria's subjects. Four decades after his first appearance in 1837, Jack attacks sentries at the army's huge Aldershot Camp. In March 1877, shots are fired at a figure who has danced about the sentry box in 'a peculiar and alarming manner'. The stranger runs off at an amazing rate. A second sentry also discharges his rifle, after his face is slapped several times by an assailant who escapes across the common 'with astonishing bounds'. Jack's reputation for being able to outrun speeding bullets isn't tarnished when it's revealed that soldiers' guns are loaded with blanks. The same year, 'Jack' is seen climbing a ruined Roman arch in Lincoln.

In reality, the explanation for all this is probably quite prosaic. The man who attacked Jane Alsop and Lucy Scales, for instance, probably knew a thing or two about fire-eating – it's not until Jane passes him the candle that his eyes glow red and he emits blue flames. If he was indeed an entertainer of some kind, he may have had access to the fancy dress he wore at the time of the assaults. Other appearances, though, seem to be the work of various nuisances.

However, if we discount the opinion of the 1961 *Flying Saucer Review*, which had its own ideas about Jack's preternatural powers and outlandish wardrobe, 'Springheeled Jack' appears to be the embodiment of Victorian society's willingness to be frightened or gulled by much that is beyond their everyday experience. The phenomenon is a reminder of the hugely different world in which Victorians lived. Their London was an ill-lit city of pea-soup smog in which policing was patchy, education scant, newspapers unreliable and the rumour mill grinding constantly. It was also a city of people making sense of a world in the throes of enormous technological, scientific, political and religious change, one in which even the educated middle-classes could be caught up in fads for seances and table rapping. Much about the old order was being challenged and threatened and perhaps phantasms, such as Springheeled Jack, can be explained in this light.

But the crimes committed during Victoria's reign that still resonate today are more serious. These, of course, are the murders by serial killers like Jack the Ripper and others whose crimes are remembered, even if their own names are not. Murder already interests one or two prominent writers but has yet to become the everyday staple of novelists and screenwriters and so real life murders, which are often sensationalised in newspapers and broadsides accompanied by gruesome illustrations, are all the more shocking. For London, the nineteenth century is book-ended by two horrific murder sprees which shock the nation to its core.

One is perpetrated by the man who would be remembered as Jack the Ripper. The other is committed by someone whose name history has all-but forgotten, but whose crimes – the Ratcliff Highway murders of 1811 – still have the power to disturb. These notorious slayings of innocent people and failings within their investigation were factors in the decision to set up a properly-organised metropolitan police force in 1829. Even though they occurred long before Victoria ascended to the throne, these crimes are worth recalling, and in some detail. What happened is this.

On 7 December 1811, at 29 Ratcliff Highway in Shadwell, in the East End of London, the Marr family are closing up their drapers and hosiery shop. For 24-year-old ex-East India Company sailor Timothy Marr, his wife Celia and their apprentice James Gowan, it's been a long day. Saturday is their busiest time and it's almost midnight before they can retire for the night. Their 14-week-old baby boy has been tucked up in his crib but before the family can turn in, there is a baker's bill to be paid and oysters to be bought. Their servant, Margaret Jewell, is despatched on the errand. By the time Margaret reaches the baker's shop on John Hill, the establishment is shut. She retraces her steps, passing the Marrs' shop and notices that Timothy Marr is still busy clearing up. Margaret tries elsewhere for the oysters, but she's too late and has to return after a wasted trip. She won't know it, but running this errand will save her life.

It's 12.20am by the time she's back at the Marrs'. Oddly, no one answers her knocks, although she thinks she can hear movement inside the house. It's the middle of the night and she's stranded on the Ratcliff Highway, certainly not the safest of the three main thoroughfares into London. She panics and knocks loudly enough to attract the attention of the area's night watchman, George Olney, who notices that a shutter is unlatched. The noise disturbs the Marrs' neighbour, pawnbroker John Murray who, (according to contemporary author Thomas de Quincey), got over a wall nine or ten feet high at the rear of the premises to see what was going on. Seeing the glimmer of candlelight through the open back door, Murray enters the house – where he gets the shock of his life. In the shop, de Quincey says, he 'beheld the carnage of the night stretched out on the floor'. According to de Quincey, 'the narrow premises so floated with gore that it was hardly possible to escape the pollution of blood in picking out a path to the front door'.

By this time a vociferous crowd has gathered with Margaret and Olney at the front door. Murray lets them in and they are silenced immediately by the 'soul-harrowing spectacle'. Just inside the door is the body of the apprentice, Gowan. The boy's head has been smashed in and his blood and brains are splashed across the floor and counter. Celia Marr is dead: her head is crushed, also. Marr has been brutally assaulted and lies dead behind his counter. Their baby boy lies in a bloody crib, his face destroyed and his tiny head partially severed.

Officers from the River Thames Police find a substantial sum of money untouched – unless the killer was disturbed by Margaret's knocking, the motive may not be robbery – and what is certainly the murder weapon, a blood-soaked maul, the long-handled hammer used by shipwrights. There is what appears to be human hair stuck to its end of it. A chisel is also found. Bloody footprints are discovered behind the shop and these are followed to Pennington Street, where it's reported that men were seen running shortly after the estimated

(*Above*) Kate Hamilton's night house, where gentlemen could meet women of easy virtue. Kate herself was a larger than life figure ("*Seated on a raised platform, with a bodice cut very low, this freak of nature sipped champagne steadily from midnight until daylight, and shook like a blancmange every time she laughed*"). (*Below*) The Kitchen in Fox Court, Gray's Inn Lane: a thieves' house and gambling den, as pictured in Henry Mayhew's *London Labour and the London Poor* (1851).

(*Above*) A cheap lodging house in the Docklands (from Mayhew's *London Labour and the London Poor*, 1851). The worst lodging houses were considered breeding grounds for disease, sexual promiscuity and crime. (*Below*) Millbank Penitentiary, built on the spot where Tate Britain now stands, owed its radical new design to the principles of Jeremy Bentham.

TICKET-OF-LEAVE MEN.
(From a Photograph by Herbert Watkins, of Regent Street.)

(*Left*) Ticket-of-leave men were prisoners released on probation. So intense was public distrust of these men that Henry Mayhew convened a meeting to draw attention to their desperate plight.

(*Right*) Early 'Peelers' were figures of fun as this 1851 *Punch* cartoon shows.

(*Left*) As Mayhew observed, children living on the streets of nineteenth century London were often forced into crime.

At the root of the early crime surge in Victorian London was the sort of poverty and urban over-population shown in this engraving of Wentworth Street, Whitechapel, by Gustave Doré (1872).

(*Left*)There was arguably more opium in middle-class Victorian medicine chests (in the form of laudanum) than in opium dens like this one, illustrated by Gustave Doré in the early 1870s.

(*Below*) London's smogs often provided cover for criminal activities in the city (*The Graphic*, 1872).

(*Above*) A ride in a prison van gave first timers a taste of life behind bars.

(*Below*) Behind Newgate's thick walls, men and women awaited transportation, or death on Monday, which was traditionally hanging day.

(*Above*) Prisoners at Pentonville were forbidden to talk to each other. The hood-like caps they wore outside prevented them communicating when exercising.

(*Below*) The unique design of Pentonville's chapel meant that even here, prisoners were unable to speak to each other – in theory, at least.

(*Above*) The burial ground and vegetable garden at Millbank Penitentiary.

(*Below*) The gothic crenellations of Holloway, then a men's prison.

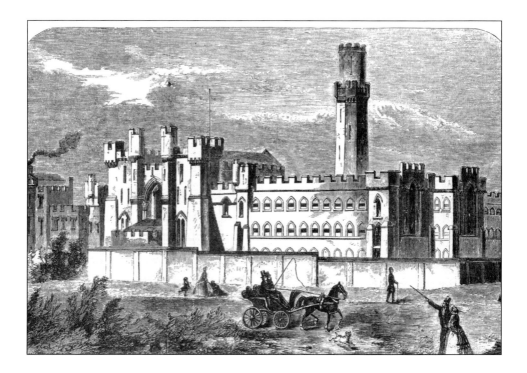

(*Above*) Picking oakum at Coldbath Fields.

(*Below*) Prisoners working on the treadmill. Prisoners dubbed this "grinding the wind" because it served no purpose other than to fatigue them.

(*Above*) Dinner is served in the oakum room of the boys' prison at Tothill Fields.

(*Below*) Silent system workshop at Millbank Penitentiary.

(*Above*) The condemned cell at Newgate. Prisoners were executed just outside the prison walls.

(*Below*) Pentonville: under the separate system, a prisoner often worked in his cell and could only communicate with prison officials.

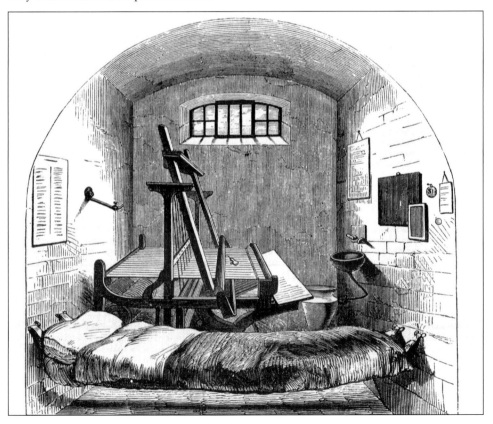

Female convicts at work in Brixton Prison, c. 1860.

The convict nursery at Brixton Prison. Finding children living (or incarcerated) within Victorian prisons was not unusual.

(*Above*) Female convicts exercising in Brixton Prison.

(*Below*) Prisoners from the hulks at Woolwich were ferried ashore to work by day. Here they are building a mortar battery.

(*Above*) The prison ship *Defence* and convict hospital ship *Unite*. The hulks were a stop-gap measure that lasted 80 years.

(*Below*) The *Warrior* prison hulk with the *Sulphur* behind. The lines of washing hanging from the masts clearly show the purpose of this ship.

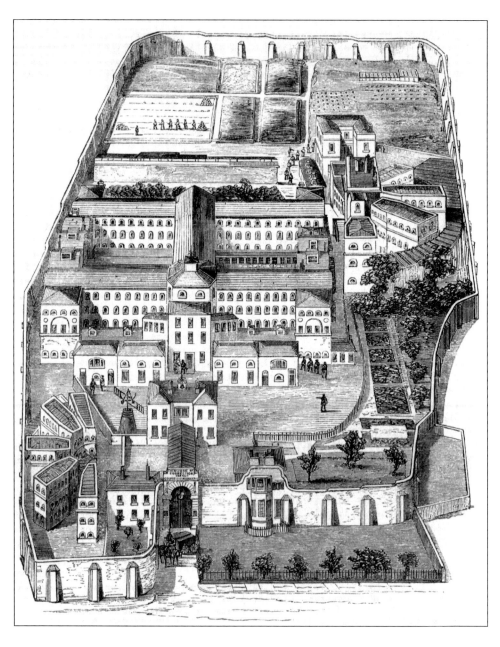

A bird's eye view of Coldbath Fields Prison.

time of the murders. Three sailors are arrested, but soon released. The bodies remain for a while in the house, where they are gazed upon by countless horrified locals.

News of this abomination spreads quickly and with it the fear that innocent people – because that's what the Marrs were, by all accounts – are not safe. Cheap publications ramp up the panic. All London is appalled at this fearful outrage. But there is little for police and the investigators hired by the church, to go on. The murders appear to be the motiveless attacks of a madman. People are interviewed and released and attempts are made to trace the ownership of the maul, whose only identifying peculiarity is a nick in the metal. The nick proves to be a blind alley and it's not until 19 December that a more distinguishing mark is noticed: the initials 'JP' carved into the handle. So much for thorough investigation. None of this is much comfort, though, to residents of Shadwell and dwellers in the low lodging houses of the Ratcliff Highway, to whom it seems that the crazed killer might strike again at any time.

Their fears prove justified on 19 December, at the Kings Arms Tavern on New Gravel Lane, Ratcliff Highway, when the publican, John Williamson, his wife Elizabeth and Bridget Anna Harrington, their elderly servant, are massacred in similar fashion to the Marrs. Not long after Williamson has asked a parish constable to keep an eye out, as he has seen a suspicious-looking man wearing brown lurking outside the pub, the cry of "Murder!" is heard. People on the street see a half-naked man scrambling from a first floor window and dropping to the road by way of knotted sheets. This is the Williamsons' lodger, John Turner. The tavern doors are opened and John Williamson is discovered, his throat cut and his head caved in and one hand severely cut. A crowbar is found. The other two occupants are quickly located, both with similar fatal injuries. The pub is searched and the Williamson's 14 year-old-grandaughter is found upstairs, miraculously unharmed.

The prime suspect at this point is a 27-year-old seaman who lodges at the Pear Tree public house, just off the Highway. His name is John Williams and he is said to have been a one-time shipmate of Timothy

Marr's. The man sharing his room at the Pear Tree noticed that he had arrived back at their room shortly after the time of the murders at the Kings Arms. But Williams is a slender man of 'pleasing countenance' and generally thought to honest. He admits to drinking in the pub on the night of the murders but claims to have been well-liked by the Willamsons.

Even so, he is incarcerated in Coldbath Fields Prison. He says that blood found on his clothing by his laundress is the result of a brawl over a game of cards. Things look even worse for Williams when the maul is traced to the trunk of a sailor now away at sea, which he had left stored at the Pear Tree. Williams has had easy access to the murder weapon. There's been no actual proof as yet, but circumstantial evidence suggests that Williams, who has never stopped protesting his innocence, is the killer.

But before Williams can come to trial, he is found dead in his cell, having apparently hanged himself with his own scarf. The Home Secretary — who doubtless wants to appear to be doing something about the grim business which has terrified and appalled London – moves quickly to tie things up. It is ordered that Williams's body should be carried through the streets of Shadwell and Ratcliff, a calming measure to prove to the credulous that the monster is no more. The cadaver is mounted on a elevated, tilted board on a cart and so is easily visible to the enormous crowds it passes through. The cart stops for ten minutes at each of the murder sites. Williams suffers a final humiliation when his body is dumped upside down into a grave dug at a nearby crossroads and a stake is driven through his heart. Many years later, a gas company excavating the site discovers Williams's skeleton and his skull finds its way on to a shelf behind the bar at the nearby Crown and Dolphin public house, from where it eventually vanishes.

The cramped confines of the capital are ideal for examining nineteenth century crime in all its multifarious forms – the resourceful London papers know what sells copies, and are full of it. Reports of petty theft, crafty swindles and forgery, violent robbery, burglaries and occasional murders litter their pages, and can give the impression that nothing much of note happens beyond its limits. So let's redress this imbalance by looking at a crime committed in Suffolk which attracts more than its share of national attention.

In fact, the Red Barn murder of 1827 is infamous the world over, having been the subject of staged melodramas, penny dreadful re-tellings and ballads. At Bury St Edmunds' ancient Moyse's Hall museum, you'll find carefully preserved relics of the murder, including pistols and a bust of their owner, the murderer William Corder, made just after his execution by hanging, showing features puffily bloated and veins swollen by slow strangulation. Yet, this is not quite the grimmest exhibit, nor does that honour go to a piece of his leathery scalp, but to a book, an account of the trial, which is bound in his skin. Exactly why we should continue to be fascinated by a murder committed almost 200 years ago in a tiny, rural village is impossible to say. But the narrative of its events reads like the plot of a good detective novel – and these won't around for another 30 years after the crime has been committed.

Born to a prosperous tenant farmer in Polstead, Suffolk, in 1804, the young William Corder is articulate and bright, but given to lying, cheating and occasional thieving, too (on one occasion, he fraudulently sells his father's pigs and on another, forges a cheque for £94). His father despairing of him, William is sent to London. Rather than finding work or going to sea, as his father hopes, Corder gets into bad company and squanders the money he had been provided with. He returns to Suffolk when he hears that his brother Thomas has been drowned while crossing a frozen pond.

Shortly before his death, Thomas had ended his affair with a pretty, local girl called Maria Martin (church records give 'Martin', not the commonly cited 'Marten') after discovering that she is pregnant with his child. The 'fallen' Maria must think herself lucky indeed when a middle-aged man called Peter Matthews decides to takes her on, if not to marry her. Thomas's child dies soon after its birth. Maria's luck doesn't hold and she is abandoned by Matthews shortly after the birth of another child. He agrees to pay a quarterly sum of £5 towards its maintenance.

Around this time, William returns from London. His circumstances have changed. His father and now all of his three brothers are dead, leaving William and his mother to shoulder the responsibilities of running the farm. This doesn't stop the slim and fashionably dressed young man looking around for distractions and soon takes up with his brother's old girlfriend. However, neither the Corders nor the Martins see much to celebrate in the renewed connection between their families. William and Maria are obliged to meet secretly, in the barn with the red-tiled roof, half a mile from Maria's house. When Maria again falls pregnant she is, of course, very keen that William should marry her. But William drags his heels and arranges for her to have the baby in a lodging house in Sudbury, nine miles distant from the censure of family and neighbours. In the event, the child dies and rather than risk exposure, William buries it in a field. It has been suggested that the child's death may not have been natural.

The couple begin arguing constantly, about the burial of the child, William's delaying of their marriage plans and about a missing five pound note, (a payment of Matthews's maintenance money). Then William appears to give in on the matter of their marriage. They will elope, he says, and wed in secret in Ipswich. They agree to meet in the Red Barn before slipping away.

In the days that follow this appointment, no one can find Maria, while William is acting is a very shifty manner. Asked repeatedly about her whereabouts, he says she's in Ipswich. Then he changes his story and insists that she's staying with a friend in Great Yarmouth. Then he announces that they've made plans to marry later that year. By September, Polstead is proving too hot for William. He flees to London and then to the Isle of Wight, writing to say that he and Maria have settled happily on the island and that Maria can't write herself, as she has hurt her hand. In another letter he expresses his disbelief that a letter from her failed to arrive.

Returning to London, William takes the unusual step of advertising in the *The Times* for a wife, and from over 100 responses, picks out Mary Moore, another 'fallen woman' he had met already on the Isle of Wight. They marry in November 1827 and soon afterwards, set up a school for young ladies in Ealing.

But William is not to be allowed to continue his new life of ease and respectability. Back in Polstead, strange events have been occurring: Maria's young stepmother tells her husband that she has been troubled by dreams. When she insists that Maria has been murdered and buried in the Red Barn, he searches the building and discovers the decomposed body of his daughter wrapped in a sack and buried in a grain storage bin. At the inquest held in the local pub, Maria is identified by the clothes she is wearing, the colour of her hair and the gap between her teeth. Tightly wrapped around her neck is a scarf said to belong to William Corder.

The cause of Maria's death isn't easy to establish: she has been shot, the ball passing through her left cheek, possibly stabbed between the fifth and sixth ribs, but has she been strangled with the scarf as well? And maybe buried alive? A capable London police officer named James Lea, together with a local constable called Ayres, trace Corder to his West London address, arresting him while he's engrossed in the business of timing his breakfast eggs. A brace of pistols is discovered, along with a French passport, suggesting that Corder intends soon to give up schoolmastering and flee the country. William Corder is returned to Bury St Edmunds to await trial.

Preparations for his trial in Bury St Edmunds attract huge and widespread interest and unmanageable crowds. Lurid accounts of the murder circulate and a journalist called James Curtis writes an account of the affair after interviewing the imprisoned Corder. Both London and the local press make a feast of the story and the murder is turned into a play even before the trial. No wonder, then, that by the time the trial opens, on 7 August 1828, the town is packed with people hoping to witness the ticket-only proceedings. It takes officials almost half an hour to negotiate the crowds outside and enter the courtroom.

Corder, looking studious in spectacles, is pale as the ten counts of murder are read out, but defends himself articulately, while complaining that the press has already condemned him as 'the most depraved of human monsters'. Circumstantial and medical evidence outweigh his defence, which includes the efforts of one or two character witnesses, and he is found guilty of Maria's murder. Corder is sentenced to death and the judge also orders that once dead, his body should be dissected and anatomised. The date of execution is set for only three days later. On Monday, 11 August, an enormous crowd – press estimates vary wildly between 7,000 and 20,000 – has gathered in the grounds beside the prison, where the gallows has been erected. A new door has been cut in the prison wall, to avoid the trouble of trying to move the condemned man through the crowds. Corder, when he appears on the platform, is ashen and has to be helped to the spot. His death is not an easy one. The executioner pulls on his legs to speed his passing, but a convulsion is recorded ten minutes later.

No one can be certain about quite what happened in the Red Barn between William Corder and Maria Martin. In a last minute confession which the prison chaplain and jailor John Orridge elicited from him, Corder claimed they had argued and his gun had gone off. He denied stabbing her (and it has been credibly argued that these stab wounds were caused by her father's mole spike, as he prodded the ground searching for her). Whether Corder is guilty of a heinous murder or only of manslaughter – having perhaps stupidly waved and accidentally discharged his gun – the Red Barn remains a compelling story of love and betrayal with a complicated murder solved by a clever detective. These elements have ensured the killing's place in the folklore of capital crime.

The matter of the dreams which uncannily led to the body's discovery are a particularly memorable aspect to the affair and it's interesting to note as a postscript that the stepmother's 'dreams' may actually have been a jealous reaction to the news that William had married Mary Moore. Maria's stepmother was only a year older than Maria and is thought to have had a romantic connection with William herself.

Few murders shock and outrage the sensibilities of late Victorians more than those of Amelia Dyer. Convicted of the murder of a single child, Dyer may be responsible for the deaths of as many as 400 children. Amelia Dyer was a 'baby farmer'. This is the term used for people who provided an answer for the difficult question of what to do with the unmarried mothers and their children who both are beyond the pale of Victorian society. For regular payments – or, preferably, a large lump sum – baby farmers will look after the pregnant mother-to-be until the child's birth. They promise then to raise the child as one of their own, thus freeing the mother of the severe stigma and encumbrance of keeping the child herself.

Few women in this position are able to find work if their situations are known and nor are they able to commit to paying a regular sum for the raising of the child. A one-off payment is more convenient, but the rates offered (between £5 and £80) won't keep a baby fed and clothed until adulthood. It's a problem made much worse by the 1834 Poor Law Amendment Act, which did away with the obligation of the fathers to contribute to their illegitimate progeny's upkeep.

Some baby farmers conclude that if the baby is neglected and then starves, then most of the payment will be saved. Before Amelia Dyer comes to this realisation, she trains as a nurse. During this period Ellen Dane, a midwife, interests Amelia in an easier way to make money. Amelia places discreet advertisements in newspapers, offering wet nursing and a caring home for infants in return for a one-off payment and the contribution of some clothing for the child. One advertisement, placed by Dyer and which results in the murder of the child, is typically innocuous: 'Married couple with no family would adopt healthy child, nice country home. Terms, £10'. We don't know when Amelia begins starving her charges, nor when she decides to accelerate the process by strangling the children with white edging tape.

Dyer's business must have been profitable. At one stage several babies were seen arriving at her door on the same day, all of whom would have been dead a short time after their delivery. However, more than the ready money attracted Amelia Dyer to baby farming. Her sadistic nature is clearly revealed in a comment she made after her arrest, "I used to like to watch them with the tape around their neck, but it was soon all over with them".

She might have continued her deadly business for years to come, had not a bargeman fished a strange package from the Thames, containing the body of a baby girl. Detectives discover the faintly legible name of a Mrs Thomas (one of Dyer's many pseudonyms). It is estimated that 20 children had been placed under Dyer's care (and subsequently murdered) in the past few months alone, a rate that leads people to consider the possibility that over the last three decades, Dyer may have murdered as many as 400 children. Dyer's plea of insanity is thrown out and in May 1896, at the Old Bailey, she is sentenced to death. The sentence is carried out by hangman James Billington, at Newgate on 10 June, no doubt to the satisfaction of readers who had been shocked and disgusted by the detailed, gruesome reports filling their newspapers, and to the relief of mothers everywhere.

But perhaps Amelia Dyer doesn't fit your idea of the archetypal Victorian murderer? Isn't that a moustachioed gent in a top hat and cape, with sharp features and piercing eyes? The sort of dastardly villain who uses his medical knowledge to slay prostitutes on the foggy streets of London? Step forward – no, not Jack the Ripper (probably not, anyway) – but Dr Thomas Neil Cream, serial poisoner, who was born in Glasgow in 1850.

Following his parents' emigration, Cream grows up in Quebec to become a man who would be labelled 'a drug fiend... a sensualist, a sadist, drug-sodden and remorseless, a degenerate of filthy desires and practises, who used his medical knowledge to slay his innocent victims'. And not by journalists on a sensationalising rag like the *Illustrated Police News* – this is the considered opinion of *The Canadian Medical Association Journal*, the organ of Cream's medical colleagues. The newspapers simply call him 'The Lambeth Poisoner'.

Dr Cream studied medicine at Montreal's McGill University, and takes his first steps towards the gallows when he very nearly kills his mistress Flora Brooks, while trying to abort their baby. The Brooks family force him to marry her, reportedly at gunpoint, but no sooner has this been accomplished than Cream takes ship for England, where he enrols as a student at St Thomas's Hospital in London. Qualifying as a physician and surgeon in 1878, he returns to Canada and starts to practise medicine in Ontario. Not long after this, a woman said to have been a lover of his is found dead behind his practice. The pregnant Kate Gardiner has died from chloroform poisoning. Creams sets a strange pattern for his future behaviour when he accuses a businessman of the killing and almost certainly tries to blackmail him. When this fails, he evades the law by absconding to the United States, where he offers abortions to Chicago's prostitutes. In the Windy City, Cream also begins to kill again.

In 1880, lack of evidence prevents a prosecution being brought against him following the death of one of his patients. Then Daniel Stott, a railway agent, and Cream's only male victim, dies of strychnine poisoning after discovering that his wife is having an affair with the doctor. Cream might have got away with this, had he not made the dangerous and incomprehensible decision to accuse the pharmacist and demand an exhumation of the body. This mistake should have ended the killings: Cream is tried and sentenced to life imprisonment. In 1891, though, he is released after a petition (and, it has been said, a large bribe), is presented to the Governor of Illinois on his behalf. Cream appears next back in London, living among the thieves and prostitutes of low-rent Lambeth. Two girls are found murdered within three weeks of Cream's arrival in England. The first, 19-year-old Ellen Donworth, dies in agony the day after being treated to a drink by Cream. Matilda Clover is 27 and her sudden death is at first thought to have been caused by alcoholism. His next victim, Louise Harris, becomes suspicious and doesn't swallow some pills that Cream gives to her. Prostitutes Emma Shrivell, 18, and Alice Marsh, 21, aren't so lucky. On 18 April 1891, they die in dreadful pain after drinking bottles of Guinness given them by Cream. The stout has been generously laced with strychnine.

When Cream accuses two doctors of killings, including the poisoning of Matilda Clover, suspicions are aroused. Until then it had been accepted that Clover's death was alcohol-related. Cream then comes under the watchful eye of the police and in 1892, having noted his habitual visits to prostitutes and learned of his crimes in America, they have sufficient evidence to charge him with the murder of Matilda

Clover. Thomas Neil Cream is tried in October, 1892 and sentenced to hang at Newgate Prison. But Dr Cream doesn't go without leaving the world another reason to remember him. According the hangman, James Billington, Cream's last words, spoken as the lever is pulled, are "I am Jack the. . .".

But Thomas Cream was not Jack the Ripper. Or at least, the probabilities weigh heavily against it. At the time of the five murders generally agreed to have been the work of this most infamous of Victorian murderers, Cream was serving what was supposed to be a life sentence, in Joliet Prison, Illinois, though for what it's worth, it has actually been suggested that Cream had a double who served time for him.

The fact is, we still don't know who Jack the Ripper was, though new theories continue to be offered up as final conclusive answers to a question left unanswered by the two police forces which investigated the murders in 1888 and the efforts of every amateur sleuth and historian since. But Jack the Ripper is important not for who he was – presumably a vicious inadequate – but for the way that the press and the public responded to the killings and created the first media frenzy to feed off serial killings.

This is a time when cheap publications have begun to proliferate, informing a wider public and competing with each other for their readers' pennies, while new printing methods allow the use of eye-catching and dramatic illustrations. The Ripper killings are manna from heaven for these rags and this makes the suggestion that some of the letters written to the newspapers purportedly from the Ripper, are actually the work of an unscrupulous journalist quite easy to believe. The story of the Ripper is a familiar one, but no account of murder on the fog-shrouded streets of London would be complete without it.

If the Ratcliff Highway murders petrified Londoners at the beginning of the century, the work of Jack the Ripper has the same effect at the end, with the difference that these murders are quickly the sensation not only of London and the British Isles, but also of places beyond these shores. The narrative of the Ripper murders is as shadowy as the Whitechapel streets in which they take place. It may be that they began before 1888 and continued afterwards – every possibility has been considered and quarrelled over in the study of these unsolved crimes. 'Ripperologists' are agreed, though, that the man the public came to call Jack the Ripper is certainly responsible for five murders in the autumn of 1888. Or three of them, at least. Ripperology is a slippery business.

The first murder generally accepted to be Jack's work can be dated to 31 August, when the body of prostitute May Ann Nichols is discovered in the early hours on what is now Durward Street in Whitechapel. It is immediately and shockingly clear that this is no ordinary murder. Nichols's throat has been cut, deeply, in two places. There are a number of cuts to her abdomen, which has been torn open. If investigators hope this is a ghastly freak occurrence, they are to be disappointed. Just a week later, in nearby Spitalfields, the body of Annie Chapman is found in a back yard. Chapman has been similarly mutilated, her throat slashed and her abdomen opened and in this case, the uterus has been removed.

On 30 September, a Sunday, two more bodies are discovered. Elizabeth Stride lies in Dutfield's Yard, Whitechapel. Her throat has been cut, but there are no further mutilations. The location, the fact that she, like all the others, was a streetwalker and the cut throat suggest that she is a Ripper victim, but the fact that she was not butchered like the others does not – unless, of course, 'Jack' was interrupted before he could finish his grim business. Shortly after the finding of this corpse, another turns up, this time not in the East End, but in Mitre Square in the City of London. Because of this, both the Metropolitan Police and the City of London police will be involved in the investigations.

Catherine Eddowes has had her throat cut and her abdomen opened. Her uterus and part of her left kidney has been removed. But the worst murder scene isn't uncovered until 9 November and it's one that must have tested the nerves and the stomachs of all who saw it. In a room at 13 Millers Court in Spitalfieds, Mary Jane Kelly's body – or what remains of it – lies on a blood-soaked bed. Kelly's throat has been very deeply cut and her abdomen ripped open. Various organs have been removed and it seems the heart has been taken away, possibly as a trophy. The hazy black and white photograph taken at the scene can only show half of the bed, which is apparently sodden with Kelly's gore and littered with her innards.

Detective Inspector Edmund Reid opens an investigation by the Metropolitan Police and is soon joined by three colleagues from Scotland Yard. Despite the limited resources and undeveloped techniques of a police force not quite 60 years old, the investigation is thorough. Over 2,000 people are interviewed and around 80 detained for further questioning. There is a forensic examination of the murder scenes and house-to-house enquiries are made in the murder districts. Because Eddowes is found in the City of London, the City Police start their own investigation and their officers also assist those of the Metropolitan force. Suspects – because of the surgical nature of some of the wounds – include surgeons and physicians. Butchers are also suspected and slaughterers of animals interviewed. Patterns in the places and dates of the killings are investigated, leading to theories that the killer might be a cattle drover or seaman.

Interest in the case explodes when letters supposedly sent by the murderer are released to the press. Of the many letters of this type received, a handful are taken seriously, three in particular. The 'Dear Boss' letter, dated 25 September and sent to the Central News Agency, earns itself some credibility when a nick is found in Catherine Eddowes's ear. A line in the letter promises to *'clip the lady's ears off'*. It's this letter which is signed 'Jack the Ripper'', gifting the press with a tradition of nicknaming serial killers which persists to this day. A postcard signed 'Saucy Jack' also contains details that only the killer should know. The series of brutal killings has an unsettling effect on the residents of Whitechapel and surrounding areas and a 'Vigilance Committee' is set up to patrol the streets. Its leader, George Lusk, is the recipient of the most ghastly of these communications. Accompanied by a letter marked 'From Hell', Lusk receives a small box containing what the letter-writer claims to be the missing half of Catherine Eddowes's left kidney.

Investigatory techniques of the time are unable to prove the veracity of the claim. The efforts of the police are exhaustive and no doubt the investigating officers come under enormous pressure to catch their man. Today DNA profiling would probably answer this riddle and locate the killer, perhaps from among the enormous number of suspects who passed through the hands of the police. Instead, the matter remains the most famous unsolved case of all. Over the course of the years, Jack the Ripper has become more than a desperate man with a knife. Part real-life ogre, part phantasm, he has shifted shape to suit the demands and neuroses of different generations, further clouding the water.

The story of this dreadful sequence of events is as popular now as ever it was, which is as mysterious to some as Jack the Ripper himself. The continuing fascination with his murderous career is clearly evident whenever his story is retold in books, dramatised on the screen or raked over in television documentaries. Is it because every story needs an end or is it suggestive of something darker? Whatever the reason, it's hard not to feel the frustration of the Victorian police as their man slips away into the mists.

But it isn't only in the murky streets of East End where dastardly murders are done. And nor are they perpetrated exclusively by the uneducated or the desperate. In Penge in South London, a murder is committed that outrages readers of newspapers, which report its every ghastly detail. It is committed by three young members of an otherwise respectable, middle-class family and the 15-year-old daughter of a publican.

Harriet Staunton is 33 when she is engaged to an auctioneer's clerk called Louis Staunton, who is ten years her junior. A surviving photograph of Harriet shows a woman who likes to dress properly, and take care of her appearance. However, by no stretch of the imagination can she be considered pretty, or an attractive prospect, especially to a man so many years younger than herself. There is something else about Harriet which might again call Louis's choice into question. Probably starved of oxygen at birth, Harriet is mentally subnormal and has the mental age of a child.

Yet, Harriet does have something that Louis needs very much: money. Harriet is an heiress to the tune of £5,000, a sum worth around half a million pounds today. Harriet's troubles begin when she meets Louis and falls for his easy charm, cheap presents and oyster suppers. Harriet's mother is at first suspicious and then alarmed at the attention lavished to her daughter. When Harriet tells her that she is going to marry Staunton, her mother tries, but fails, to have her declared a lunatic and made a ward of court. All this time, Louis Staunton is continuing to see his 15-year-old sweetheart, Alice Rhodes.

Very probably encouraged by Staunton, Harriet leaves her mother's care and goes to live with an aunt, at whose address Louis continues to court her, and to see Alice Rhodes. Harriet's mother, deeply concerned about her daughter, pays her a visit and is given what she concedes is a civil reception. However, shortly afterwards, she receives a letter from Harriet, whose perfect spelling indicates that it was written under someone else's direction. In it, she tells her mother not to come again, in case it causes 'a disturbance' between herself and her husband.

After a short engagement, Louis and Harriet marry. Louis then buys Little Grays farm, which is situated in a secluded spot in Cudham, Kent, a short walk from the cottage that is home to his brother Patrick and his wife Elizabeth – Alice Rhodes's sister. After Harriet gives birth to a boy, she and the child Thomas are moved into a bare upstairs room in Patrick's ramshackle and isolated cottage. There is nowhere for her to wash and the bed is only boards on trestles. Her outdoor clothes and jewellery are taken away from her.

In a letter to Alice Rhodes, Louis writes, 'there will be a time when Harriet will be out of the way and we shall be happy together'. Meanwhile, Alice is wilfully forgotten, as she stays imprisoned in her room, scratching at lice, moaning and slowly starving to death. Her screams – perhaps when Patrick strikes her for trying to escape – are heard by an agricultural worker, who unfortunately dismisses them as wind in the treetops. The mindsets of Patrick and Elizabeth, who sleep so close to her, and Louis and Alice, who must hear her scratching and wailing when they visit, is very hard to imagine.

Harriet's mother tracks her down to Kent but is forbidden to enter the house. She has no idea of what is being done to her daughter behind the door that is closed in her face. When baby Thomas is clearly dying, Louis takes him to Guy's hospital, concocting a cock-and-bull story to explain the child's emaciation and bruise on his cheek. Shortly afterwards, when Harriet too is obviously at death's door, she is taken to a lodging house in Penge, where she dies. The doctor ignores (or is too incompetent to recognize) the clear signs of starvation and, as a later inquest records, 'dirt which had to be scraped off like the bark on a tree'. He decides she has died of apoplexy, or suffered a stroke.

However, when the husband of Harriet's sister hears Louis Staunton recording her death, (he happens to be standing behind him in a post office queue), he becomes suspicious and the police investigate. Louis Staunton, his brother Patrick and Patrick's wife Elizabeth and Alice Rhodes are charged with murder. When the trial comes on, it is a sensation. The middle-class spectators, who treat it like a social occasion, will already have digested countless lurid reports of Harriet's lingering death in the press and will perhaps have seen some of the imaginative illustrations, too. There is no doubt a frisson of excitement to be enjoyed: the Stauntons are not quite comfortably and respectably middle-class, but they have pretensions. A photograph of Louis and Alice shows a young man with deep-set eyes and a moustache, dressed in his best three-piece suit and watch chain. Standing at his side is the rather vacant-looking Alice, who also is dressed rather well and very probably on Harriet's money.

London is outraged by the cruel murder, which somehow seems so much closer to home. Harriet died not in Whitechapel or Stepney, or the Ratcliff Highway, where such things are almost to be expected, but in suburban, middle-class Penge. In his defence, Louis Staunton claims that Harriet was an alcoholic, who wouldn't eat the food he prepared for her and that Harriet died from tubercular meningitis. Found guilty, all four defendants are sentenced to hang.

But just two days before the scheduled executions, the Home Secretary bows to pressure exerted by the medical profession, which has been outraged that certain medical evidence presented at the trial had been dismissed out of hand. Louis, Patrick and Elizabeth Staunton have their sentences commuted; Alice Rhodes is released. Patrick will die in prison of consumption at 28, while his wife will be released in 1883. Louis becomes a model prisoner who attends mass in the prison chapel every Sunday. He maintained, even to the day of his release in 1897, that Harriet was an alcoholic who refused her food. The truth of the matter will never be known. Whether this was a matter more of wilful negligence than premeditated murder and whether once again, the press had a hand in the trial's outcome, are questions that remain unanswered.

When schoolteacher Julia Martha Thomas is murdered in 1879, Londoners are aghast — and for two good reasons. Firstly, the 54-year-old Thomas ("a small, neat lady" according to her doctor) has been murdered by her Irish maid, 30-year-old Kate Webster. At this time, the fear of attack by one's own servants is very real and one which prompted an enormous crowd to turn out for the execution of Francois Courvoisier, 40 years earlier. The valet had murdered his aristocratic employer in his sleep. But Kate Webster has not only killed her own employer, she also dismembered and boiled down the body and disposed of it in a box which she dropped into the Thames.

After two weeks in which she poses as Julia Thomas, Webster gives herself away and immediately flees to Ireland, where she is arrested at the home of her uncle, in County Wexford. Her trial at the Old Bailey attracts huge interest. While Madame Tussauds jumps the gun and produces a waxwork figure of the defendant, spectators at this sensational prosecution include the Crown Prince of Sweden. Public opinion is strongly against Webster from the start. Rather than appearing frail and emotional, she is dour and stoic, and described as "a tall, strongly-made woman". She has a history of criminal behaviour and sexual promiscuity and has previously been imprisoned for theft both in Ireland and England. Her public image isn't helped by the lurid stories and graphic illustrations which appear in sensation-seeking publications such as the *Illustrated Police News*.

If any small thing can be said in Kate Webster's favour it's that her life has been a hard one. Like the rest of the vast female servant class, she has been paid poorly and has had low expectations of anything better. Also, Julia Martha Thomas may not have been the perfect employer. Described as a woman of "excitable temperament", she regularly found cause to criticise the standard of Webster's work. The relationship between the two women had become filled with resentment, distrust and, on the part of Julia Thomas, of fear, too. This culminates in Thomas serving Webster with her notice. 'Gave Katherine warning to leave', reads her last diary entry.

When Webster's late return from a local pub delays Thomas's departure for a church service, the women quarrel violently, Thomas telling a member of the congregation that her servant has "flown into a rage". Webster maintains her innocence throughout her trial, but on the eve of her execution, she confesses that later that same evening, "Mrs Thomas came in and went upstairs. I went up after her, and we had an argument, which ripened into a quarrel, and in the height of my anger and rage I threw her from the top of the stairs to the ground floor. She had a heavy fall, and I became agitated at what had occurred, lost all control of myself, and, to prevent her screaming and getting me into trouble, I caught her by the throat, and in the struggle she was choked, and I threw her on the floor".

It is what Kate did next which was so appalls the country: "I determined to do away with the body as best I could", Webster says. "I chopped the head from the body with the assistance of a razor which I used to cut through the flesh afterwards. I also used the meat saw and the carving knife to cut the body up with. I prepared the copper with water to boil the body to prevent identity; and as soon as I had succeeded in cutting it up I placed it in the copper and boiled it. I opened the stomach with the carving knife, and burned up as much of the parts as I could".

Webster puts as much of the body as she can fit into a box and asks the son of a neighbour to give her a hand to lift the weighty box down to the Thames, where, unseen, she drops it in. The box is discovered the next day by Barnes Bridge. The contents are at first taken to be butchers' off-cuts. Julia Thomas's head remains undiscovered for another 130 years, when workmen, building an extension to naturalist David Attenborough's house, unearth it in his back garden.

During her trial, Kate Webster tries to avoid her fate by first implicating three innocent men and then, when asked if she has anything to say before sentence is passed, claims to be pregnant. This throws the court into confusion. The judge, at a loss as to how to proceed, at last invokes an ancient legal device called a 'court of matrons', to decided if Kate Webster really is pregnant. A panel of women, and, in this case, a doctor, is convened to physically examine the prisoner. It doesn't take long for them to decide that Kate is not pregnant. Kate Webster is sentenced to death and hanged three weeks afterwards, by William Marwood, using his new 'long drop' method, at Wandsworth Prison.

In this case as in many others, the threatening of the rigidly stratified social order plays a considerable part in the public and media perception of the crime. If servants can murder their masters or wives kill their husbands, then who is safe? This is still a churchgoing society which has yet to omit the verse in *All Things Bright and Beautiful,* which suggests that the class system is ordered by God:

> *The rich man in his castle,*
> *The poor man at his gate,*
> *He made them, high or lowly,*
> *And ordered their estate.*

It's also a time when a man's wife is subject to his law and (although magistrates generally disagree) there is a general acceptance that he's within his rights to administer the odd 'correctional' beating. With servants being paid so little and wives so treated, it's perhaps not surprising that danger is perceived from both servants and women and this (perhaps guilt-tinged) fear sometimes weighs in the pressing of prosecutions on less-than-perfect evidence.

High on the list of contenders for the nineteenth century's most notorious murderer is a Staffordshire doctor. Born in 1824, William Palmer qualifies as a physician in 1846, but his generally dissolute lifestyle leads him into debt and he uses his medical knowledge for heinous ends. Although Palmer is eventually tried and convicted of only one murder, that of a rich friend called John Cook, he will be suspected of planning and carrying out the murders of members of his family and others, usually for the sake of the huge amounts of money for which he has insured their lives.

Soon after Palmer marries Ann Thornton, his mother-in-law comes to stay. She is the beneficiary of a bequest thought to total the enormous sum of £8,000. As the law stands, any money that her daughter inherits in the event of her death will become the rightful property of her husband. Two weeks after arriving at the Palmers' household, she is dead. An elderly doctor records her death as having been caused by 'apoplexy'. It comes as a grievous shock to Palmer when the inheritance turns out to be much less than he expected.

Palmer gambles at the racetrack and a man from whom he borrows £600, dies mysteriously at his house. Heavily in debt and forging his mother's signature to pay off creditors, Palmer takes out a life insurance policy on his wife. When Ann dies at the age of 29, her death is ascribed to an outbreak of cholera. Four of her five children have already died, apparently of 'convulsions'. But the money paid out to Palmer doesn't last long. Facing ruin and the debtors' prison, Palmer insures the life of his brother Walter, an alcoholic. Plied with bottles of spirits, Walter dies but, after so many deaths in the family, this time the insurance company smells a rat and investigates.

Palmer at this time is planning the murder of John Cook, a racetrack friend with a large inheritance. Palmer may have been poisoning Cook over a period of time. Celebrating a win on a horse, Cook complains that his brandy is burning his throat and tells his friends of his suspicion that Palmer has been 'dosing' him. Cook becomes sick again at a later meeting with Palmer, after having unwisely accepted a bowl of soup. He dies in agony the following day.

Despite Palmer doing his best to interfere with the post-mortem, the inquest jury decides that Cook has "died of poison wilfully administered by William Palmer". The doctor is arrested and because the local press is having a field day with the case of 'The Prince of Poisoners', new legislation is enacted which allows Palmer to be tried at the Old Bailey in London, where the trial is unlikely to be so prejudiced. The bodies of Palmer's wife and brother are exhumed and examined. Two chemists admit selling strychnine to Palmer, who claimed he needed it to poison a dog. The jury deliberates for just an hour before returning a 'guilty' verdict. On 14 June 1856, a crowd of some 30,000 watches Palmer hang outside Stafford prison.

And then there are those who – just possibly – get away with murder...

Florence Maybrick, the daughter of a banker, was brought up in an antebellum mansion in Mobile, Alabama. After the death of her father, 19-year-old Florence Chandler, with her mother, embarks on a transatlantic steamer bound for England. During the six day crossing, she meets and is courted by James Maybrick, 42, a Liverpool cotton merchant. Despite the age difference, Florence and James are married in Piccadilly and begin their new life together at Battlecrease House, just outside Liverpool.

The cotton magnate and his young American wife must seem a glamorous couple when they appear at balls and social events in Liverpool, but at home in Battlecrease House, it's a very different story. James, Florence discovers, has his ways. He is addicted to arsenic, for one thing. In very small, soluble doses, this notoriously poisonous substance has been used as a stimulant since the mid-18th century. James may be using it to feed an addiction which began when arsenic was prescribed to him after he contracted malaria. (Victorian women used arsenic for another reason: white arsenic mixed with chalk and vinegar produces the pale complexion much in vogue at this time.)

The Maybricks' is a messy, unhappy marriage from the start. Neither partner is faithful to the other: James keeps several mistresses, while Florence has liaisons of her own. James's brother Edwin becomes one of her lovers, but it's after James discovers that Florence has been seeing a local businessman, that a furious row ensues, during which Maybrick assaults Florence and tells her he will sue for divorce.

When James falls dangerously ill, apparently after dosing himself with a poison, Florence's habit of buying arsenic-impregnated flypaper is called into question. After James dies, in May, 1889, his brothers, whose suspicions have been aroused by arsenic found in a bottle, have his body examined. Although the amount of arsenic found in his system would have been insufficient to kill him, Florence is tried for murder at St George's Hall, Liverpool. In a statement read out at her trial, she claims that her intentions were innocent: "The flypapers were brought with the intention of using as a cosmetic", she says. "Before my marriage, and since, for many years, I have been in the habit of using a face-wash prescribed for me by Dr Greggs, of Brooklyn. It consisted principally of arsenic, tincture of benzoin, elderflower water, and some other ingredients. This prescription I lost or mislaid last April, and, as at the time I was suffering from slight eruption of the face, I thought I should like to try to make a substitute myself. I was anxious to get rid of this eruption before I went to a ball on the 30th of that month". The jury isn't convinced by this and, despite reasonable grounds for doubt, Florence is sentenced to death.

There is doubt over the conviction and a public outcry. The pretty young American is spared the gallows, her sentence commuted to one of life imprisonment. After 14 years spent in prisons in Woking and Aylesbury, Florence is released. Did Florence murder her husband? It might be argued that he had given her sufficient grounds but Maybrick's will would not have made her a rich woman. Only Florence knew and when she dies a penniless hermit, in 1941, she takes her secret to the grave.

Doubt also hangs over the result of the trial of Adelaide Bartlett, a strikingly pretty French-born woman whose motives for marrying the wealthy but unhealthy and decidedly odd Thomas Bartlett might well be questioned. Bartlett had rotten teeth and, quite possibly, tapeworms too. Other aspects of the marriage were highly unusual. Adelaide had an affair with the couple's spiritual, councillor, a Reverend George Dyson, apparently encouraged by Bartlett. The will made out by Bartlett, in which Dyson was appointed executor and everything left to Adelaide, was changed four months before he died in mysterious circumstances. Whether Adelaide knew that, isn't known. What is known is that that Adelaide sent George to buy more of the chloroform which had been prescribed to treat Bartlett for subacute gastritis and, seemingly to avoid the necessity of signing the poisons book (necessary in the purchase of large quantities of such substances), he bought four small bottles, each from a different shop.

After Thomas Bartlett dies, his stomach is found to contain a lethal amount of chloroform. What puzzles the examiners is just how it got there. Liquid chloroform burns the throat and no signs of any such burns were found. It didn't seem at all likely that Bartlett had somehow managed to gulp it down so quickly that he avoided harming his throat and larynx. Nor, as he had ordered a lavish dinner to be cooked for the next day, did claims of suicide seem credible. But no suitable explanation was made and no evidence presented in regard to how the poison found its way into Bartlett's stomach.

And so, after a strong defence from Sir Edward Clarke, one of the best criminal lawyers then practising, the jury acquits Adelaide Bartlett, but not without expressing its unease in doing so. Members of the jury believe that murder has been committed, the foreman says – they just don't know how. Adelaide Bartlett, it seems, has gotten away with murder.

Soothing Syrups and Cocaine Toothache Drops

If Victorian society has its problems with drink – on the one hand the gin palaces and the other a growing temperance movement – it also has trouble with drugs, though the use and sale of these is legal and unregulated for more than half of the century. On a national scale, these problems are writ large. China's refusal to allow British ships to supply a demand for Indian opium, created by the British themselves, sparks the first of two opium wars. Domestically, the problem with drugs is insignificant when set against rampant alcohol abuse, but it is surprisingly widespread.

In the Victorian household, opium is much in demand, albeit qualified with alcohol and taken in the form of laudanum. While the press sensationalises accounts of depraved Chinese and Lascar sailors smoking opium in East End padding kens, the drug quietly finds its way into the medicine chests of the middle-class too. Laudanum, which contains around 10 per cent opium, is seen as a universal panacea. In an age when doubtful medicines and snake oil cures pushed by street hucksters claim to cure everything from liver disease to cancer, laudanum is actually an effective painkiller and a useful treatment for diarrhoea.

The drug is sold as an essentially wholesome remedy. Advertisements of the time depict children playing happily under the slogan *Cocaine Toothache Drops, Instantaneous Cure,* while *Mrs Winslow's Soothing Syrup, the mother's friend for teething children,* contains an unspecified dosage of morphine. In his *Great Wen* blog, Peter Watts notes that London was awash with opium, 'in pubs, chemists, general stores and markets, where it was sold in bottles, powders, pills, lozenges, on plasters, in sweets and much else besides. The centre of trade was in Mincing Lane, London, where 90 per cent of transactions occurred. It was most commonly taken as laudanum, a tincture of opium and red wine, with saffron and cinnamon'.

If raw opium is tainted with connotations of the mysterious and un-Christian Orient, laudanum is still quite acceptable and, like opium, freely available. This is the case until the Pharmacy Act – which does no more than limit its sale to qualified pharmacists – is introduced in 1868. Earlier in the century, poets and writers such as Samuel Taylor Coleridge and Thomas de Quincy had been notable users of opium. Now, laudanum plays a part in the lives of eminent Victorians too. Its use kills Gladstone's young sister and very probably is responsible for the death of the artist Dante Gabriel Rosetti's second wife and long-time muse, Lizzie Siddal. While the drug is a handy treatment in the days before aspirin and other painkillers, it isn't immediately realised that regular use can lead to addiction and debilitation.

Problems with the use of opium become evident in the most unlikely of places. Karl Marx claims in *Das Kapital* that 'in the agricultural as well as the factory districts of England, the consumption of opium among adult workers, both male and female, is extending daily'. There are even accounts of workers in the Fenlands adding opium to their beer. In a report of the Medical Officer of the Privy Council, 1863, prompted by 'the excessive mortality of infants in some rural districts of England', a Dr Hunter reports the following state of affairs: "A man in South Lincolnshire complained that his wife had spent a hundred pounds in opium since he married", he says.

"A man may be seen occasionally asleep in a field leaning on his hoe. He starts when approached, and works vigorously for a while. A man who is setting about a hard job takes his pill as a preliminary, and many never take their beer without dropping a piece of opium into it. To meet the popular taste, but to the extreme inconvenience of strangers, narcotic agents are put into the beer by the brewers or sellers." Opium usage in the Fens is thought to be attributable to the native maladies of these wetlands, "ague, poverty and rheumatism".

Chloral, (or chloral hydrate) is a popular drug used by insomniacs and others. Rosetti takes it mixed with alcohol, which contributes to hallucinations and a mental breakdown. Cannabis, also found to be a useful treatment for a number of conditions, is prescribed to Queen Victoria herself for the relief of menstrual cramps. And there are reports of a young Winston Churchill taking cocaine lozenges or gum with the Queen while staying at Balmoral.

PUNISHMENT

'Help, Police!'

Despite all the pickpockets, muggers and swindlers on the streets in mid-century and the continued existence of areas in which criminals consider themselves safe from interference, things might have been a lot worse. By this time Sir Robert Peel's Metropolitan Police, at first suspected as an infringement of civil liberties and then made the butt of jokes, has effected a marked decrease in measurable crime rates and people are said to feel safer on the streets and sleep better in their beds. A whiskered constable patrolling his beat is now a common and reassuring sight in the city.

This new police force comes into being after Peel pushes through the Metropolitan Police Act of 1829, and changes the way Britain deals with law-breaking and civil disturbance for ever. There was policing before 1829, but this was a piecemeal system made up of parish constables and often old and doddery watchmen who received little pay and consequently often proved useless in emergencies. In London, there were the thief takers known as Bow Street Runners, a force which had been set up by the novelist and Chief Magistrate Henry Fielding, in 1749.

In times of civil disturbance – and the early nineteenth century has more than its share, with violent industrial unrest and major campaigns for political reform – a magistrate is called to read the Riot Act before setting an armed militia loose on the crowd. In 1819, 15 people are killed in the so-called Peterloo Massacre at Manchester, when cavalry charge a crowd with their sabres drawn. The congregating of some 60,000 protesters on St Peter's Fields is only one of a number of factors making the property-owning and power-wielding classes nervous. They see the working-class as a dangerous, even a criminal class. Up North, Luddites are breaking machines and fighting with the military. And then there are Britain's troubles abroad, many of which might be laid at the door of radicalism which has gone unchecked – the American War of Independence and the French Revolution in particular.

All of this means that there is more to Peel's bill than simply the prevention of crime. To some extent, the new police is there to keep a lid on sections of the populace who might prove troublesome or even dangerous if left uncontrolled. London itself seems dangerous. Scattered around the city are areas such as Saffron Hill and Alsatia (between Fleet Street and the River), parts of South London and, of course, the notorious St Giles, where it is (probably rightly) considered unsafe to set foot. After a stuttering start – the very first police officer, who bears the number 'one' on his collar, is sacked after only four hours for being drunk on the job – the new force goes to work. Dressed in serge tunics which are blue to avoid military connotations, the 'Peelers' or 'Bobbies' wear sturdy top hats which protect their heads and can be stood upon for a slightly elevated view. They carry 'bullseye' lanterns and are armed only with truncheons. If assistance is needed, they can summon another officer with a rattle. Further distancing themselves from the military – at a time when commissions are bought and sold – the Metropolitan police can be promoted only on merit.

They work out of police stations in one of the 17 divisions into which London is initially divided. The jurisdiction of the Metropolitan police is a radius of seven miles from Charing Cross, but by 1836, this had been extended to 15. Also divided is public opinion of the new force. As Richard Gaunt says in *Robert Peel and the Metropolitan Police*, 'persons of small property, such as shopkeepers and artisans, seem to have welcomed the new protection against crime and disorder as readily as did the well-to-do. Working people were more suspicious of interference, and in some industrial areas, open hostility to 'Bourbon police' was to outlast Peel's lifetime'. Henry Mayhew notes that anything about the police gets people talking and records costermongers' opinion of the force after an incident in which 'two or three policemen, with their bulls eyes...and still more effective truncheons' had 'speedily restored order':

111

"The blessed crushers is everywhere," shouted one. "I wish I'd been there to have a shy at the eslops", said another. And then a man sang out:"O, don't I like the Bobbys?"

The CID is set up in 1844, following public outcry at a particularly brutal murder, and receives a mixed reaction, too. The plain-clothed detectives are considered sneaky, unsporting perhaps, even by fellow policemen: according to *Punch*, the ordinary constable considers the wearing of plain clothes 'unperfessional' [sic].

For *Punch,* policemen are easy figures of fun. A piece entitled 'The Model Policeman' has a constable popping up whenever food appears. 'He keeps his eyes straight before him,' says *Punch*, 'even if there is a leg of mutton from the baker's running the opposite way'. The model policeman 'is rather particular in seeing if the coal cellar is fast, about supper-time'. He's not proud, they allow, and in an emergency will hold a gentleman's horse and only 'take sixpence for it'.

In fact, the Metropolitan policeman earns his money. Many of Mayhew's accounts of burglaries and other incidents are attended by police with amazing speed, suggesting that one at least can usually be found quickly. This may be because by 1865 the Metropolitan Police, (excluding the 608-strong independent City Police force), numbers 6,295 constables, inspectors and superintendents and the main force of constables spend their time on the beat, not behind desks.

But the policeman's lot is not always a happy one. His shifts are often 12 hours long and he's paid from 14s to 22s weekly, although his uniform is free and he gets an allowance of candles and coal. A constable taking a night shift can find himself pacing up and down streets from nine in the evening until nine in the morning in all weathers, checking doors and windows and dealing with every kind of incident, from drunken brawls and petty thefts to housebreakings by armed gangs.

As well as deterring crime by their presence on the streets and checking the security of premises as they do so, the first Metropolitan police officers inherit the work previously performed by the watchmen. They light lamps, call out the time, keep a look out for fires and try to oblige anyone with a reasonable request for assistance. They get to know their beats well, and the faces of troublemakers and lawbreakers too. Initial hostility in areas such as Seven Dials becomes a grudging respect when it's realised that policemen will investigate thefts and break-ins and try to settle disputes there as well as in the monied districts of the city. Numerous reports of the time praise the force for bringing some measure of stability to London's turbulent streets.

CHAPTER 5

'From the Hulks!'
Prison life, afloat and ashore

A fearful man, all in coarse grey, with a great iron on his leg. A man with no hat, and with broken shoes, and with an old rag tied round his head. A man who had been soaked in water, and smothered in mud, and lamed by stones, and cut by flints, and stung by nettles, and torn by briars; who limped, and shivered, and glared and growled; and whose teeth chattered in his head as he seized me by the chin.

(Charles Dickens, *Great Expectations*, 1861)

Should you find yourself – for whatever reason – out on the lonely Essex marshes across from Woolwich, you will see an extraordinary sight, though it's long been familiar to people living in the isolated villages on this shore and to the workers in the Royal Arsenal on the other. Out in the river lies a small fleet of warships at anchor. Frigates and 74 gun ships of the line float where they were anchored decades ago, and though it is said that some of these ships have an honourable history, their current condition offers no hint of former glory. Stripped of masts and rigging, timbers rotting, nothing more exalted than lines of washing hang from their spars now. These are the hulks, the prison ships feared by Pip and his family in *Great Expectations*. "I wonder who's put into prison ships and why they're put there?" Pip asks after his first encounter with the convict Magwitch and it's a good question.

The reason for the mooring of these ships off Woolwich (and at Chatham, Portsmouth, Plymouth, Sheerness and Bermuda, too) is Britain's loss of its colonies following the American War of Independence, after which the practise of dumping convicted felons on the American shores is brought to a sudden end. Over 40,000 convicts have been transported there up to this point, but now the door is firmly closed. Criminal practises continue, however, leaving the Government with the problem of what to do with a growing number of convicts and nowhere to put them.

Until now, the prisons have been used as a holding measure, places to keep petty malefactors for short periods or more dangerous law-breakers between conviction and transportation, or execution. And so, in 1776, as a purely temporary measure intended to last no longer than two years, a couple of old warships are requisitioned and stationed off Woolwich, where it will be possible to use the prisoners as free labour at the Royal Arsenal and to assist in dredging of navigable channels in the river. It is stop-gap measure, but one that will last 80 years.

Warship prisons must have seemed a brilliant idea at first. In service they would have provided accommodation for a crew of several hundred – now, with their guns and all unnecessary features removed, they can be packed with men, until some other provision can be made for them. The first two prison ships, the frigate *Censor* and the *Justitia* ('an old Indiaman'), are soon joined by more and the fleet is augmented by a hospital ship, the *Unite*, and the *Sulphur*, a laundry ship where the prisoners' soiled clothes can be washed and mended.

Although transportation of convicts to New South Wales begins in 1787, the use of prison ships continues. They provide a handy interim solution while transportees await their places on the convict ships and besides, there is a lot of work to be done in the yards of 'the Warren', 'a labyrinth of workshops, warehouses, barracks, foundries, firing ranges and mountainous stacks of oak, teak and pine spread along the Woolwich shore'. By the mid-1800s, the *Justitia* had been replaced by a new namesake and the *Defence* and the *Warrior* ('patched up as well as her unsoundness will permit' claims a report) have been recommissioned for this purpose.

Life aboard the prison hulks is unremittingly grim, especially in the early days. Only two years after the first ships are commissioned, a government inquiry is convened to look into deteriorating conditions. The penal reformer John Howard manages to get the food improved, if only slightly, with mouldy green bread and hard brown biscuit eventually being replaced by a more varied diet of barley or rice soup for breakfast, meat (often bullock's head) and beer for lunch and soup or porridge for supper. As well as the daily allowance of beer, there is doubtfully-filtered water from the river. But poor food isn't the worst of the conditions a prisoner endures aboard the hulks.

The ships provide accommodation on three decks and in specially-built bunkhouses. Each deck is divided lengthways into cells. A 'tigers' den', a heavily barred area, is provided for the most dangerous inmates. Prisoners are allocated a deck according to their behaviour, the worst occupying the lowest deck, the best behaved the top. All the prisoners sleep in hammocks, which are stowed away before they disembark for their daily shore duties. The ships are massively overcrowded. In 1841, some 3,000 men are accommodated in just a dozen prison ships, nine of which are anchored in British waters, the other three lying off Bermuda.

In the *Justitia*, 500 men are supervised at night by a single warder, leaving the weak at the mercy of the predatory. The young are especially vulnerable. John Binny, Mayhew's colleague who diligently looked into prison conditions, records the ages of prisoners aboard the hulks: three are under ten years old; 213 are aged 10-15; 958 are 15-20; 1,630 are aged between 20 to 30; and 839 are older. One prisoner is recorded as being 80 years old. The youngest inmates must feel they are being thrown to the lions.

Disease, in such overcrowded spaces, is rife. Sanitary conditions are poor, even aboard the hospital ship *Unite*. Water closets stink and overflow. The close confinement of prisoners and poor ventilation, especially on the lower decks, encourages the spread of maladies. In 1841, the surgeon of the *Warrior* reports 400 admissions to hospital and 38 deaths. Binny (and possibly Mayhew) paints a telling picture in *The Criminal Prisons of London*, when he writes of being *assured by one of the warders, who had served under the old hulk regime, that he well remembers seeing the shirts of the prisoners, when hung out upon the rigging, so black with vermin that the linen positively appeared to have been sprinkled over with pepper; and that when the cholera broke out on board the convict vessels for the first time, the chaplain refused to bury the dead until there were several corpses aboard, so that the coffins were taken to the marshes by half a dozen at a time, and there interred at a given signal from the clergyman; his reverence remaining behind on the poop of the vessel, afraid to accompany the bodies, reading the burial-service at the distance of a mile from the grave, and letting fall a handkerchief, when he came to "ashes to ashes and dust to dust," as a sign that they were to lower the bodies.*

The prisoners' daily regime is a hard one. James Hard Vaux, a prisoner aboard the *Retribution* in the early 1800s, remembers that every morning, at seven o'clock, "all the convicts capable of work, or, in fact, all who are capable of getting into the boats, are taken ashore to the Warren, in which the Royal Arsenal and other public buildings are situated, and there employed at various kinds of labour; some of them very fatiguing; and while so employed, each gang of sixteen or twenty men is watched and directed by a fellow called a guard".

Sometimes it isn't only the guards who watch; the prisoners are something of a local tourist attraction, at times attracting crowds of interested onlookers. As well as stacking mountains of timber and cleaning rusty shells, the shackled prisoners make mortar, break stones and assist free men (who sometimes assist in freeing prisoners) to do whatever is necessary in the always busy Arsenal. Some prisoners work on nearby garden plots, but the produce is generally appropriated by the officers on board. Vaux recalls the guards as being "commonly of the lowest class of human beings; wretches devoid of feeling; ignorant in the extreme, brutal by nature, and rendered tyrannical and cruel by the consciousness of the power they possess".

These guards, he says, "invariably carry a large and ponderous stick, with which, without the smallest provocation, they fell an unfortunate convict to the ground, and frequently repeat their blows long after the poor fellow is insensible". Discipline is harsh on board the ships too. Though 'mild and persuasive means of correction are tried at first', the *London Illustrated News* of 1846 reports, punishments are then a 'reduction of allowance of provisions, confinement in a dark cell with no other food than bread and water, for not more than seven days' or 'moderate whipping, which, in any case, is not allowed to exceed twenty four stripes'.

But sometimes the work itself is fearful. John Binny draws our attention to the sheds where the notoriously unstable military rockets are made. These rocket sheds, he says drily, "are rather celebrated for accidents". The governor of the Arsenal has been telling him that "occasionally you see the men at work there, rush out with their clothes all in flames, and dive into the canal". Only a month or so ago, he admits, "two or three sheds blew up, and the rockets were flying about all amongst my men". As Binny passes, "a workman, black as gunpowder, appeared at the door of one of the sheds".

Meanwhile, in a yard off London's Caledonian Road, men in brown hoods are walking silently in circles. On closer inspection, you'll find these aren't really hoods at all, but brown caps of an unusual design. The caps have strange peaks that hang so low over the face that only the eyes of these men are visible, as they peer out through slits made in the cloth. Dressed identically and with blinkered vision, it's doubtful whether one man can recognise another. No one speaks and the only sound is the tramping of feet and the commands of the man who stands outside the ring and is their guard. The large and forbidding edifice behind them is Pentonville Prison, the latest manifestation of new and enlightened thinking on what an ideal prison should be.

At the turn of the nineteenth century, a convicted prisoner, trembling in the dock at the conclusion of his trial, will have been expecting the judge, having donned the black cap, to sentence him to be publicly hanged or to be exiled from his country and kin for perhaps

14 years. For the courts, death and transportation are the main punitive options. However, by the early nineteenth century, there is a growing unease about the enormous number of capital crimes on the statute books, and rather than doom the accused to a grisly death on the gallows, increasingly, juries are finding prisoners, 'not guilty' and quite often, it's not only the innocent. Transportation will continue long after this particular issue has been resolved, yet by the middle of the century, this too is being seen (not least by Australian settlers) as a far from ideal solution to the problem of what to do with Britain's convict population.

It's hard to imagine now, but just then, the idea of using gaols as places for convicts to serve out their sentences is a new and radical one. Up until this point, the country's ramshackle collection of lock-ups, small county gaols, crumbling old Elizabethan houses of correction and the eyesore that is Newgate have been used as holding centres. They were places to confine the accused awaiting trial, to keep undischarged debtors until they had settled their debts and to provide temporary accommodation for those awaiting transportation or execution. The trouble is that while crime now appears to be increasing alarmingly, the number of capital crimes has been reduced to a mere handful and there's only the prisons and the hulks in which to house a growing population of convicted felons.

The prisons as they stand clearly aren't up to the job. These overcrowded, dark, filthy breeding grounds for 'gaol fever' are, as often as not, run by corrupt and venal administrators. There is no separation of prisoners according to the severity of their crimes, and most spend their time gambling, playing pitch and toss, boasting of their crimes and getting drunk. Rather than being in any way reformatories, these are colleges of crime in which first time offenders can easily become lifelong recidivists. In 1836, prison inspectors visit Newgate. In the yard, the inspectors see "associated together the convicted and the untried, the felon and the misdemeanant, the sane and the insane, the old and young offender". And once inside, it's soon clear to them how the prison operates: "In ward No10, we found that the wardsman, a convicted prisoner, owned all the bedding, the crockery ware, the knives, forks, kettles and saucepans, for the use of which each prisoner pays him 2s 6d per week".

At least prisoners have free access to reading matter. "There was a good supply of Bibles and prayer books", the inspectors report, although "These books, particularly the Bibles, bore little appearance of having been used". Cupboards are opened for them, in which they find pastimes more to the tastes of the inmates:

> *we discovered a pack of cards, apparently much used, a cribbage board and pegs and two draughts boards and men. We also found four tobacco pipes...and a box of tobacco. These, though forbidden by prison regulations, were quite exposed on the shelves of the cupboards and must have been detected on the most superficial inspection of the ward by any officer of the prison.*

Something must be done and it is decided that the new prisons springing up in the capital will be run along very different lines. Prison design is the first big difference. Prisons such as Millbank, (built where Tate Britain stands now), and Pentonville, rather than having communal wards and yards, will be cellular. Ideally, each prisoner will occupy a cell of his own. This design paves the way for the implementation of two new systems, both designed to minimise communication between prisoners and so lessen the chances of old lags corrupting first offenders and less seasoned criminals. It's envisaged that these new prisons will be reformatories, where the prisoner has some chance of taking up an honest life after leaving.

As well as a new method of classification, in which prisoners will be categorised according to age, sex and crime, prisons begin to experiment with the 'silent' and 'separate' systems. Under the first regime, which has already been tried out in American penal institutions, prisoners are kept in solitary confinement until transportation and only allowed communication with their warders or the prison chaplain. Their days are passed in complete silence. Initially, prisoners can expect to spend 18 months in these conditions before they are expatriated to Australia. Under this silent system, men are made to work but are prohibited from communicating with each other by word or sign.

The sudden imposition of the silent system must have come as a rude shock to inmates such as those at Coldbath Fields Prison, where, says Mayhew, "It was introduced...on 29th December 1834, on which day, 914 prisoners were suddenly apprised that all communication by word, gesture or sign was prohibited. Without any approach to overt opposition, the silent system became the rule of the prison". Although early reformers believe that this new system will lead to reflection, penitance and reform for prisoners – hence the term 'penitentiary' – there are others who see inherent problems from the start. In 1842, Charles Dickens visits a prison in Philadelphia in which prisoners are kept in silent, solitary confinement. "I hold this slow and daily tampering with the mysteries of the brain to be immeasurably worse than any torture of the body", he pronounced.

And, of course, the imposition of complete silence on such a large group of men who by definition can be unruly is far from easy. It's soon discovered that preventing a large prison population from talking to each other requires "an inordinate number of officers" and although outwardly it might seem to be working, prisoners are still managing to communicate by subtle signs, murmurings in church services or by pointing at numbers scrawled on walls.

Pentonville opts for the separate system instead. Called the 'Model Prison', its arrangement of tiered cell blocks radiating in a semi-circle from a hub will indeed be the model for over 50 more prisons just like it. The separate system confines the prisoner to a cell which becomes his workshop by day and his bedroom by night. In some cells, the prisoner may find himself sharing cramped space with a loom. At exercise he wears the brown cap, which prevents him from communicating with other inmates, and he attends Sunday services in an extraordinary chapel fitted out with tiered rows of coffin-like boxes in which each prisoner's separation from the next is preserved. Systems such as these are difficult to police and there is a constant stream of inmates appearing in the governor's office who have been reported for

121

breaking the new rules. Transgressors are punished with reductions in their food allowance, a bread and water diet or with a spell in a 'black hole', dungeon-like cells in which the offender might spend two or three days in complete darkness. In the end, it will transpire that neither system is a complete success, and the number of instances of men being driven insane by their solitary condition is such that the time a man must spend before transportation will quickly be halved.

A common sentence handed down by the courts is one of 'hard labour' but when prison administrators find that interpretations of what constitutes hard labour can differ wildly, an attempt at standardisation is made. This takes the form of a set of activities designed to punish and physically tire the prisoner and to instil in him the habit of labour. While some prison activities have a clear point to them – scrubbing floors or sewing, for example, or even stone-breaking and 'picking oakum' (the painstaking separation of strands of tarred rope for use in caulking ships), the treadwheel, the crank and the shot drill have none.

Unravelling prison life

Picking oakum is tedious,wearing and not for anyone who prides themselves on their cuticles. But at least this activity has a use. The tarred rope which is painstakingly unravelled by prisoners is used to caulk the joints of timbers in ships of the Royal Navy. In the mid 1800s picking oakum is a common occupation for prisoners. According to John Binny, writing in *The Criminal Prisons of London*, prisoners have to pick around 2lbs a day, unless sentenced to hard labour, when they might be expected to pick up to 6lbs in a day. " Each prisoner has by his side his weighed quantity of rope", Binny says.

Some of the pieces are white and sodden-looking as a washerwoman's hands, while others are hard and black with the tar upon them. The prisoner takes up a length… and untwists it, and when he has separated them into so

---

> *many corkscrew strands, he further unrolls them by sliding them backwards and forwards on his knee with the palm of his hand until the meshes are loosened. Then the strand is further unravelled by placing it in the bend of a hook fastened to the knees and sawing it smartly to and fro, which soon removes the tar and grates the fibres apart...all that remains to be done is to loosen the hemp by pulling it out like cotton wool and the process is completed.*

The treadwheel is introduced after the governor of the new prison at Bury St Edmunds complains to the renowned civil engineer William Cubitt about his inmates "lounging idly about". Although its revolutions might usefully have been harnessed to grind corn or pump water, the instances of the treadwheel being used for such purposes are few and far between. Mostly, the prisoners striding the steps of Cubitt's invention 'grind the wind'. At Coldbath Fields, Mayhew says, 'there are six tread-wheels, four in the felons' and two in the vagrants' prisons. Each of these is so constructed that, if necessary, twenty four men can be employed on it', although, he adds, 'the present system is for only twelve men to work at one time. At the end of a quarter of an hour, these 12 men are relieved by 12 others, each dozen hands being allowed 15 minutes rest between their labours. During this interval the prisoners off work may read their books or do anything they like, except speak with one another'.

Mayhew being a fiend for detail, offers his observations and measurements of the wheel itself: 'Each wheel contains twenty four steps, which are eight inches apart' he says, 'so that the circumference of the cylinder is sixteen feet. These wheels revolve twice in a minute and the mechanism is arranged to ring a bell at the end of every thirtieth revolution and so to announce that the appointed spell of work is finished. Every man put to labour at the wheel has to work for fifteen quarters of an hour every day'. Mayhew works out that each man must climb 7,200 feet daily.

It's not a pleasant way for prisoners to pass the time; men complain of being stifled and not all can stand the exertion. 'Those who have never visited a correctional prison can have but a vague notion of a treadwheel', Mayhew says. 'The one we first inspected at Coldbath Fields was erected on the roof of the room where the men take their meals. The entire length of the apparatus was divided into 24 compartments, each something less than two feet wide and separated from one another by high wooden partitions, which gave them…the appearance of the stalls at a public urinal'.

The appearance of the men themselves suggests to Mayhew 'the idea of a number of squirrels working outside rather than inside the barrels of their cages'. The work is heavy, repetitive and slow: 'those labouring in the boxes on the wheel were lifting up their legs slowly as a horse in a ploughed field, while the thick iron shaft of the machinery, showing at the end of the yard, was revolving so leisurely that we expected every moment to see it come to a standstill. We soon learnt that "grinding the wind" was such hard labour that speed could not be given to the motion of the machine'. The men coming down from the machine have flushed faces 'wet with perspiration'.

Such is the onerous nature of working on the treadwheel that prisoners resort to 'numerous subterfuges' to avoid it. 'Either they feign illness or maim the body', Mayhew says, noting that the prison surgeon records 3,972 cases of such 'feigned complaints'. Water is limited, because men have used it to "disorder the system", the prison governor says. Salt, too, has to be watched, otherwise prisoners will swallow "inordinate saline solutions," to give themselves a stomach disorder. Soap can be made into pills and taken to provoke diarrhoea, lime applied to the tongue or "any available rubbish bolted" to bring on a temporary bout of sickness. If the inmate is found by the surgeon to be shamming, he is sent back to the wheel but if he continues to complain, he risks being assigned to the crank and, Mayhew says 'after a couple of days at this employment, the most stubborn usually ask to return to their previous occupation'.

The crank is as pointless (and perhaps as soul-destroying an activity) as stepping up the treadwheel. The device Mayhew sees looks like a knife grinder, he says, a 'narrow iron drum placed on legs with a long handle on one side which, on being turned, causes a series of cups or scoops...to revolve'. Inside the machine is a thick layer of sand which the scoops carry to the top of the wheel and empty, providing resistance for the handle. The amount of resistance can be adjusted by the turning of screws, a task that the warders attend to and which is thought to be the origin of the term 'screws', the slang for prison warders. Prisoners are expected to turn the crank around 10,000 times a day, and some prisons withhold meals until the machine registers the requisite number of revolutions. Although at least one prison harnesses the power the turns generate, using it to operate a saw and make firewood, mostly the exercise is hard, dispiriting and achieves nothing.

But the punishment which seems to take most out of its recipients is the shot drill. Up to 57 men can be punished at once, lining up in a three-sided square in a yard reserved for this purpose. The activity itself consists in picking up pyramid-stacked shot – cannonballs the size of coconuts but very much heavier – and then walking three yards before lowering the ball to the ground and building a new pyramid of shot. The exercise is then repeated once in the other direction. The balls are sufficiently weighty to make repeated stooping and lifting tell on neck and shoulder muscles. 'The men grew hot and breathed hard', Mayhew observes. 'It tries them worse taking up, because there's nothing to lay hold of', a warder tells him, 'and the hands get hot and slippery with the perspiration, so that the ball is greasy like. The work makes the shoulders very stiff, too'.

Even if the assigned work isn't as onerous as these exercises, its unfamiliarity can cause problems for some. Gentleman convict Jabez Balfour:

> I do not suppose I had ever done any sewing in my life. After breakfast, some heavy canvas was tossed into the cell, a ball of thread, with a lump of wax and two large needles were handed to me and I was told to begin to sew it as strongly and as neatly as I could. I was also shown

how to wax my thread. My only other appliance was a thimble. It was hard work in more ways than one. Until I had threaded a needle with that thread I had no idea how difficult it is and I am afraid I spent the greater portion of that first day in trying to overcome that initial difficulty.

However inhumane the restrictions on communication and however pointless and arduous the work, it's not hard to see why the separate system endures. To an observer, the prison must present an orderly, even peaceful appearance and the standards of cleanliness achieved by having the prisoners scrub and clean every day make the places seem modern and progressive and light years advanced from the barbarity of ages past, relics of which can be seen in the fetter room at Millbank. John Binny is shown its contents by a warder:

It was one of the ordinary cells, but literally hung in chains, which were arranged against the walls in festoons...In front of the window there was set out a fancy pattern of leg-irons, apparently in imitation of the ornamental fetterwork over the door of Newgate. The walls glittered with their bright swivel handcuffs like stout horses' bits...

But the brilliancy and lightness of some of the articles were in places contrasted with a far more massive style of ironmongery, which appeared to have been invented for the Cornwall giants. A few of the manacles...were as large as the handle on a navigator's spade and there were two massive ankle cuffs, with chains...weighing something more than twenty-eight pounds. There were neck pieces too, heavy enough to break an ordinary collar bone, whilst everything was on so gigantic a scale that we were struck by the absurdity of such monstrous contrivances...

Still there was something too real about the scene...to induce any but the grimmest smiles, for by the side of the colossal swivel-cuffs, figure of eight cuffs and iron waistbands...there were little baby handcuffs, as small in compass as a girl's bracelet, and about twenty times as heavy – objects which impressed the beholder with a notion that in the days of torture, either the juvenile offenders must have been very strong or the jailers very weak, otherwise where was the necessity of manacling infants?

The warder tells Binny that "We never use anything here but a single cuff and chain" and appears to regret recent moves towards more humane regimes. "It's given up everywhere now", he says, "except in Scotland...The prisoners who come to us from Scotland have leg-irons and ankle cuffs and the cuffs are fastened on them so tightly that the people here have to knock away at them for some time with a heavy hammer before they can drive the rivets out. Occasionally, the hammer misses...and hits the man's ankle".

But although prisoners are no longer regularly manacled, the courts still have the power to impose sentences of corporal punishment. Flogging isn't common, but is considered by many to be a suitable addition to a prison sentence for perpetrators of brutal crimes, such as garroting. In 1874, James Greenwood reports on the flogging of two men at Newgate prison. Entering the prison, Greenwood very nearly collides with William Calcraft, the elderly hangman, who is also responsible for carrying out sentences of flogging. "The British public are not favourably disposed towards the lash, except in extreme cases", but there is unlikely to be an outcry about the punishment of the two young men who are to be strapped to a frame and flogged on this day.

The first "assaulted a lady in broad daylight", Greenwood says, "and after partly strangling her, had seized her watch-chain, and tugged at it with such brutal determination, that his victim's throat was seriously lacerated. This promising young fellow, aged twenty-two, had been previously convicted, and his sentence was two years' hard labour and twenty-five lashes with the cat". The second is named as 'Regan' and worked in the vicinity of Borough High Street. "While in pursuit of his peculiar trade", Greenwood says, "a female confederate had entrapped a wayfarer into the mouth of an alley; and while she was holding him in converse Regan, the garrotter, pounced on him, and in two seconds had his murderous thumbs on the man's windpipe. Somehow, there was a struggle, and to make sure of his prey, Mr Regan flung him down on the stones, and, to make surer still, kicked him about his defenceless head with his hobnailed boots. It wasn't of the least consequence to him where his iron-shod boot-sole alighted, so he kicked the poor wretch in the face as well, and knocked his eye out; thus when the wounded man was discovered, the maltreated organ of sight was lying on the man's cheek".

Now, in a bare, whitewashed room, the witnesses have assembled. Standing with Greenwood are "one of the Sheriffs, Mr Bennett", the prison governor, "several other gentlemen and, most important of all, the doctor". The men are to receive 30 lashes each, which, we are told, "form an exceptionally severe flogging". Greenwood says that in Russia, men have been known to die "under the infliction of the knout" so "why not under the thong of the much-dreaded cat?"

First to be flogged is Regan, whose face, Greenwood is pleased to note, bears "an expression of terror". Regan, he reports, is a "brawny-shouldered, well-nurtured ruffian, with a bullet-head, and a chin deeper and broader than his forehead; a muscular young fellow, standing five feet eight or so". His shirt, which had been hung loosely on his back is now stripped off, revealing goose-pimpled flesh. "He was in a mortal fright, but he said nothing", Greenwood says, only "uttered a muffled snort, like a horse with his head in a nose-bag". Greenwood is clearly disappointed in the appearance of the small whip which Calcraft now produces and suggests that had Regan been able to turn and see it, he might have laughed. Greenwood describes the instrument as "nothing more than the handle of a hearthbrush, and a penn'orth of string of the thickness of a tobacco-pipe…The handle was about two feet in length, and the 'tails' about fourteen inches".

Calcraft spits on his hand and makes a start. Greenwood says he isn't surprised that Regan does "not writhe or yell, or utter any agonised exclamation" because, in his opinion, "there was nothing to yell about…the hangman might as well have flogged a brick wall for any cry of pain that was elicited from the sturdy young garotter". After another ten stripes, "Mr Regan was flogged out of his determination to 'take it dumb' and…growled out 'Oh!'". After the fourteenth or fifteenth blow, Greenwood says, "the punishment began to tell and Regan cried out 'Whooo!' and 'Ah!'but it was behind clenched teeth and in not at all a loud tone". Greenwood continues:

> *About the eighteenth lash he turned his face to the hangman, and said, in tones of reproach rather than entreaty, 'Lay it on fair, will yer?' and then planted his forehead against the board to take the other twelve. When he had received them, from under his left shoulder-blade to the top of his right there was an ugly beer-coloured patch about six inches in width but he was not made to bleed at all, and when his limbs were released he needed no assistance in putting his shirt on. Reckoning from the moment Mr Calcraft spat in his hand until now, exactly a minute and three-quarters had elapsed.*

The second man "came up smiling and pulled off his shirt as though about to engage in a bout of boxing" and for "three, four, five" strokes, made no sound, though he 'writhed and winced". He too asked the hangman to "lay it on fair" and "at every stroke, he arched his back and twisted his head backwards with a sudden jerk, as though to look at the smarting place. He didn't yell, but he suffered so much more than Regan that the hangman…feelingly apologised for his share of the business", advising his victim not to make it worse for himself by struggling.

Though Greenwood professes to "hope never again to witness such a performance", he leaves the prison less shocked by the spectacle itself than by the half-hearted manner in which it has been carried out. His final words hit home with his readers:

> *"I have no idea who prescribes the size, weight, and pain-inflicting properties of the Newgate cat, or whether the judge*

who passes the awful sentence ever asks to see the instrument with which it is to be carried out. If neither of their Lordships has done so yet, I would humbly advise them to make the inspection without delay. The very cat with which the ruffian Regan, and after him Lily, were lashed, might, without fear of shocking them, be laid before them, and that just as it was when its frightful work was done, since its every tail was clean and white, and as free from crimson stain, as when the hangman brought it out of his cupboard.

I hope that I am not one who delights in the utmost rigour of the law; indeed, it is my opinion, that, as a rule, transgressors are too severely punished but, at the same time, I have no hesitation in declaring that it would be a salutory amendment if the Newgate cat were made at least twice as formidable as it is at present. Undoubtedly it inflicts considerable pain – the discoloured backs and subdued moans and mouthings of the two men I had seen were sufficient proof of that; but more than this is needed. It is generally understood that the application of knotted thongs to the bare human back is productive of a spell of agony so intolerable that the mere threatening of it acts as a check against men of such devilish inclinations even as Regan.

The law and the people tolerate the use of the dreadful cat-o'nine-tails only because they believe that the worst of criminals, such as garotters, are more afraid of it than of Portland slavery or solitary confinement; and, supposing the lash to be real and not make-believe, the conjecture is correct. It is a fact that Regan, with all his brute strength and barbarous recklessness, dreaded Saturday morning so much that several days before he pretended illness, and would have been content almost to live on physic for a time, if he could have shirked the punishment which he had heard was so terrible.

But can any one believe that the brute who could stamp on a fellow-creature's head for the sake of the few shillings in his pocket, was tormented through the day, and haunted through the night, by imagining the sort of scourge that the hangman whipped him with? There can be no doubt that his horrified mind pictured an instrument many times more severe, and it is an injustice to those who rely on the law for protection that his tormenting bodings were not amply justified by the result.

It is to be hoped that the convict Regan will be the last who will be able in truth to tell his comrades, that the much-dreaded lash – at Newgate at least – means nothing more than a whip of string which does not hurt more than a birch rod, wielded by a man whose arms have grown feeble with age, who commiserates those on whom it is his duty to carry out the law's just sentences, and who furnishes them with valuable hints against their hurting themselves more than in the tenderness of his heart he would.

Prompted by the appearance of this article in the *Daily Telegraph,* an inquiry is held, resulting in the standing down of the feeble Calcraft. Warders will carry out future floggings, with a whip more likely to strike fear into the hearts of anyone toying with the idea of making garotting or other thuggery their choice of career. Jabez Balfour, a Liberal MP and financier sentenced to 14 years for his part in a financial scandal in 1892 which left thousands penniless, says the anticipation of the flogging is the real punishment. "God forbid I should make light of the mental agony which any man must suffer who is doomed to undergo this distressing experience", he says, "However hardened, however depraved, however brutal such a man may be, his mind must inevitably dwell on the ordeal which is before him. The punishment of the lash is inflicted in a few moments but in those few moments are concentrated the emotions, the sufferings and the fiendish passions of a lifetime".

And, although Balfour says that care is taken that "no prisoner shall see, or, if possible, hear anything that is going on", prisoners evidently did hear what was going on. The fact was known to everyone, he says, recalling the "kind of awe-stricken silence and stupor" which settled on the prison whenever a flogging was to take place.

For Balfour, who published a serialised account of the long stretch he served at Pentonville, Parkhurst and Portland prisons, punishment comes in a subtler form. In a society with rigid class divisions, being thrown into the company of common(er) criminals is like being outcast from civilisation. It's a shock he first experiences on being led into the Black Maria transporting him from court. "I found the vehicle was packed with the refuse of the London police courts", he says. "They apparently knew each other very well and were on most excellent terms of friendship with their guardian, who walked up and down the corridor and chaffed them unmercifully, especially the female prisoners".

It's a ride through London which, he says, he will never forget. He's offended by the oaths and obscenities he hears, "a sensation almost of suffocation in the tiny closet in which one is confined", but it's the social disaster which he finds most humiliating. "To a man of refinement", he complains, "the sudden association, on terms of equality...with the noisy and ribald dregs of criminal and outcast London is an experience calculated to beget despair in the most sanguine mind".

Despite experiences of this kind, Balfour offers a surprisingly even-handed account of life in various Victorian prisons. He has a lot of sympathy for the warders who do, as he sees it, a difficult job in difficult conditions, and recalls "the extraordinary kindness towards prisoners that is shown by most prison officials". In fact, Balfour seems to go out of his way to cast the whole system in as good a light as he can shine on it. Holloway, which has yet to become a women's prison, is "not as bad as I expected". Perhaps he's remembering his early days on remand, when he was allowed to rent a room which was "barely but not uncomfortably furnished" (and which he paid another prisoner 6d a day to clean and tidy) and had his meals sent in from outside. But this isn't to say that flaws in the system escape his attention.

There's the matter of hygiene, in particular. "A large proportion of the inmates of Pentonville belong to the 'street arab' class of the population and they are as filthy in their personal habits as they are lawless and debauched in their lives", he writes. "Every time that one of these London pariahs enters the prison, he brings with him on his body, in his hair and on his clothes, quite a devastating horde of abominable parasites. He is literally laden with them". In prison, he says, dirt dominates. It's no wonder prisons aren't as clean as the might be, he says, when "neither the clothes that the prisoners wear nor the cells they occupy, nor the halls in which they are housed can by any flight of fancy be regarded as clean".

Partly, he says, this is the fault of the conditions in which the prisoners are housed. Although prisoners are expected to scrub out their cells once a week, the lighting is too poor for the prisoner to do a thorough job. The cell is lit by "a single jet of gas placed in one corner of an oblong vault, the light from which is dimmed by the thick and frosted glass that screens it". Then there's the equipment. The small cube of soap which is served out to prisoners fortnightly, he says, is just enough for a man to wash his face and hands twice a day and for his weekly bath, but doesn't leave much for scrubbing out his cell.

Nor is he impressed by the cell itself. His accommodation at Portland on the Isle of Wight is "a box seven feet long, seven feet high and four feet broad'. Despite being a small man, he can touch the ceiling with his hand. For furniture, he has a wooden stool, a tiny flap table and a hammock. It is, he says, "nothing but a small, corrugated iron kennel with a stone or slate floor." And, like so many inmates before and after him, he loathes one feature above all:

I observed in the door of the cell a small hole, a kind of peep-hole and from time to time, I could see an eye applied thereto watching me closely. All that night, as I lay awake, turning restlessly on my narrow plank bed, it seemed to me that the unpleasant sense of being watched would prevent me ever sleeping at all in prison, but one gets used to that as to almost everything else in life.

A Debt to Society

It was an oblong pile of barrack building, partitioned into squalid houses standing back to back, so that there were no back rooms; environed by a narrow paved yard, hemmed in by high walls duly spiked at top. Itself a close and confined prison for debtors, it contained within it a much closer and more confined jail for smugglers. Offenders against the revenue laws, and defaulters to excise or customs who had incurred fines which they were unable to pay, were supposed to be incarcerated behind an iron-plated door closing up a second prison, consisting of a strong cell or two, and a blind alley some yard and a half wide, which formed the mysterious termination of the very limited skittle-ground in which the Marshalsea debtors bowled down their troubles.

(Charles Dickens, *Little Dorrit*, 1857)

Not all the inmates of British prisons have picked pockets, burgled houses, committed highway robbery or worse. Some are confined without hope of release only because they have incurred a debt. There are many likely reasons why a person might end up in a debtors' prison, not least the increasing practise of buying on credit. Debt is classless. The middle-class man furnishing his house improvidently is as likely to end up behind prison walls as the reckless spendthrift, the hopeless gambler or the victim of one of the many ingenious scams practised at all levels of society. In these days, the man of the house is responsible for financial matters and can end up in prison if his wife overspends.

The original sum might have been quite small, but the overseers of these run-for-profit debtors' prisons soon ramp up the amount due with charges for rent, food, linen and levy all sorts of other spurious fees, sucking their luckless inmates into a vortex of ever-increasing debt. Debtors in London's Marshalsea, King's Bench, Fleet prisons and other places of detention live according to their means. Those with money (an anomalous position for a debtor, surely?) can hire their own apartments and use other facilities, such as a bar or a restaurant, or they can lounge in the prison yard. Those without money enjoy more rigorous conditions and many resort to begging alms from passers-by in the street, who might sometimes slip a farthing or a halfpenny through a grille in the wall. This is at least a small improvement on the preceding century, when hundreds of imprisoned debtors starved to death.

Incredibly, some prisoners of the Fleet Prison are not required actually to live in the gaol, but can rent accommodation within a specified distance of the prison, a curious practise known as 'Liberty of the Rules'. This freedom depends on a sizeable payment (yet another bribe) being made to the gaoler. Other prisoners are allowed out in the day, ostensibly so they can repay their debts, in reality so that they can maintain their payments to the prison authorities. The rest linger inside the walls, hoping for a miracle. It is hard to imagine the frustration, the longeurs and the despair suffered by the inmates living under this mismanaged and pointless system.

But the law is merciless and blind to the predicament of the debtors. Nothing mitigates the debt, neither a small total amount, nor the fact that the debtor might have done what he can to repay it. Lawyers do little more than add their fees to the amount owed. It's not only debtors themselves who suffer because of this. We would find it more than strange today to see children in prison with their parents, but in the debtors prisons of the early 1800s, whole families are held together, when the wives and children are incapable of supporting themselves after the breadwinner has been incarcerated.

If you discount the money-grabbing gaolers, imprisonment for debt does no one any good. The prisoner is bled of income and made unable to repay the original debt, and the party to whom he owes money will be very lucky to get paid. It's not until the Debtors Act of 1869 that imprisonment for debt is finally abolished.

CHAPTER 6

The Rope's End
Yhe long and short (drop) of capital punishment

On a windy, wet morning in April 1800, a slight girl with large, child-like eyes mounts a cart in the market town of Bury St Edmunds, in Suffolk. She is 21-year-old Sarah Lloyd, a house servant said to be "a decent individual of good character". The cart is taking Sarah to a site outside the town, where she will be hanged for the theft of two pounds' worth of trinkets and a watch.

As the cart wheels jolt over the cobbles, she appears to be remarkably composed, holding an umbrella to protect herself from the inclement weather. At Tay Fen fields, the execution site, a large crowd has gathered to see Sarah's final moments and they are not all are there for the sake of ghoulish entertainment. Sarah's predicament has become something of a *cause célèbre*, evidenced by the presence of a peculiar-looking man who stands in the wagon at her side.

This is Capel Lofft, a middle-aged lawyer whose boyish face and squeaky voice are becoming well-known in London's political and literary circles. He's here now, though, as a local magistrate of independent means. While the hangman lingers over his preparations – apparently unsettled by Sarah's composure – Capel Lofft makes a five minute speech in which he denounces the government and what he sees as a travesty of justice – and wins the support of the crowd. Lofft must know that his inflammatory words will lose him his position as a magistrate, but Sarah's case has excited his passions. Besides, there is something unusual about this wide-eyed girl – whom previous employers have tended to treat as one of the family – which has appealed to the sensibilities of both Lofft and her jailor, the forward-thinking prison governor, John Orridge,

As Sarah adjusts her hair so that hangman can settle his noose, let's consider the facts as Lofft sees them. What has happened is this: while working for a Mrs Sara Syer of Hadleigh in Suffolk, Sarah falls under the influence of a plumber and joiner called Joseph Clark. He promises to marry her, but Clark's attachment seems to have been formed for his own purposes. He wants to rob Mrs Syer and fatally Sarah agrees to go along with his plan and lets Clark into her mistress's house, where the trinkets are stolen and a small fire is started in the stairwell.

They immediately flee the scene. The fire is quickly extinguished by neighbours and after the briefest of searches, Sarah is discovered at her mother's house, which is only streets away. Sarah might have been tried on counts of attempted murder, arson and burglary, but the prosecution at the next Assizes decides to try her on the easiest of these to prove, the theft of the trinkets. For reasons which remain unclear, Joseph Clark, very much the instigator of these crimes, is acquitted, while Sarah is condemned to death. Lofft is horrified by such an injustice and campaigns on Sarah's behalf, firing off letters to the press, soliciting the help of influential figures and getting up a petition.

Capel Lofft is already a controversial figure, supporting a string of radical political causes, from American independence and the French Revolution to the nascent anti-slavery movement. Here, perhaps he sees not only a chance of saving a wronged and helpless girl, but the opportunity of making changes to the system of judicial punishment known as the Bloody Code. After long years in which some 200 crimes, many as paltry as Sarah's, were punishable by death, the Code is on its last legs and might just need one last push. A change is in the air and one which will affect the way crime is dealt with in the new century. But none of this carries any weight with the Duke of Portland, the Tory Home Secretary, who has confirmed the order for Sarah's execution, on the grounds that 'the object of punishment is example'.

A change in the system at this time would have seemed a mad, dangerous move by many, the property-owning classes in particular. The last 30 years have been tumultuous and have seen too many people upsetting the social order and forgetting their places. The American colonists have snatched their independence while the French middle and lower classes have usurped the nobility and allowed a dangerous general called Napoleon Bonaparte to seize power. Sarah's sentence may well have been a draconian reaction to all of this. But the fact that she too has upset the order of things by attacking the home and person of her employer would certainly have sealed her fate. And so Sarah dies. She makes the fatal signal herself; the cart moves off and Sarah pitches forward. After a minute, she moves her hands to her chest, twice, and then is still.

Two hundred years of polluted weather have all but erased the epitaph of Sarah Lloyd, which you can see on the wall of the charnel house in the graveyard of St Mary's Church in Bury St Edmunds, in Suffolk. You need to look closely to make out these words:

Reader, pause at this humble stone. It records the fall of unguarded youth, by the allurements of vice and the treacherous snares of seduction. Sarah Lloyd on the 23rd April 1800, in the 22nd year of her age suffered just but ignominious death for admitting her abandoned seducer into the dwelling house of her mistress on the night of 3rd October 1799 and becoming the instrument in his hands of the crimes of robbery and house burning. These were her last words 'May my example be a warning to thousands.

Sarah Lloyd would have drawn little comfort from the knowledge that she is playing a small part in a slow movement of change and that the first decades of this new century will see reductions in the enormous number of crimes punishable by death, discretionary powers handed to judges and alternative approaches to dealing with matters of crime and punishment. Whether these new methods will be any more successful remains to be seen, though, and as the century gets into its stride, it's evident that the gallows isn't going short of victims.

Hanging is rough justice. Until the general introduction of the long drop, the condemned are turned off ladders, or are left suspended as the cart which has carried them to the gallows moves off. Alternatively, they fall through traps with unmercifully short drops. In all cases, the person hanged is strangled to death, a process that can take several minutes, unless the hangman, or the victim's relatives and friends, choose to speed his end by hanging on his legs. Until leg restraints are introduced, it as not unusual to see the man 'dancing the Tyburn jig' as he struggles for life. Hanging will remain the ultimate sanction until the 1960s and executions will still be bungled even after the introduction of the neck-breaking long drop. However, the ritual of capital punishment in the latter half of the nineteenth century is at least an improvement on the bloodshed throughout the previous hundred years.

Public executions in the eighteenth century are as much spectacle and theatre as easily-intelligible warnings to a largely illiterate population on the consequences of crime. Tyburn's 'triple tree', a towering triangular gallows, which can be seen at a distance from whichever of the three roads you approach it by, does furious business in the 1700s, to the noisy gratification of the boisterous crowds of apprentices, hawkers, tradesmen and others who have shirked work on a 'hanging Monday'. The better-off pay a shilling apiece to sit in the tiered bleachers known as Mother Procter's Pews. Tyburn is black carnival and one in which entrepreneurs do a brisk trade. Food and drink is sold while broadside sellers try to interest customers in a printed account of an execution (often containing the condemned's last dying words) which has yet to happen. This is the scene awaiting the men, women and sometimes young teenagers who are to die here today.

For these people, the fatal drama will have begun on the last day of the Sessions, when the judge, wearing the nine-inch square of black silk that denotes the passing of a sentence of death, will have condemned whole batches of prisoners at once. Death sentences are mandatory for a staggering range of crimes. This comes in the wake of the 'Black Act', a knee-jerk piece of legislation rushed in as a reaction to a series of raids carried out by gangs of poachers in Hampshire and Windsor Forest. The Blacks, or Waltham Blacks, as they are variously called, have been poaching deer on a large scale, going out at night with blackened faces to avoid recognition. They seem to be products of straitened times but their choice of targets – a park belonging to the Bishop of Winchester and, finally, a shipment of wine destined for the Prince of Wales – are perceived as being deliberately provocative and the bill that is enacted is aimed directly at putting an end to this sort of depredation.

After 1723, anyone caught 'going Armed in Disguise and doing Injuries and Violence to the persons and Properties of His Majesty's Subject' can be speedily and effectively punished. Anyone with a blackened face found in a chase, down or Royal Park might now be hanged. Similarly punishable are various other rural crimes, such as fishing, catching hares, and setting fires. Following the Act, there are 50 more crimes for which a person might be hanged. By the turn of the nineteenth century, there are around 200 capital crimes on the books.

So, standing in the eighteenth century dock might be sheep stealers, pickpockets, burglars, highway robbers, rapists, sodomists and, in theory anyway, someone who has kept company with gypsies for one month. Once the judge has pronounced the dread sentence – that they will be returned to the prison from whence they have come and taken from there to a place of execution where they will be hanged by the neck until dead – the prisoners are kept on a diet of bread and water in conditions often so filthy that convicts are known sometimes to die in the cell rather than on the gallows.

On hanging day itself, prisoners are taken to the Press Room where their fetters are knocked off with a hammer, before being loaded onto carts for the two mile, two-hour journey to Tyburn. The procession to the gallows is one of the more macabre sights of eighteenth century London life. Depending on how they are perceived by the crowd, the condemned, as they rattle slowly along the streets, guarded by a troop of javelin men, might have to endure constant barracking and even hurled missiles. En route, the cart stops at a pub, where the prisoner is allowed a last bowl of ale and the procession pauses again at a church. Some of the condemned wear their best clothes for the occasion, while others, probably wanting to deprive the hangman of his right to the clothes of his clients, do not. Some prisoners make a show of bravado and play to the crowds, but they are the exceptions. The death that awaits them can be a slow and painful one.

Beyond pulling on the legs of the hanged, the hangmen do little to ease the passing of their charges. Some are reportedly drunk as they adjust the noose and others are clearly incompetent. Perhaps it's not so surprising, then, that there are instances of people surviving. It is usual for the bodies of the hanged to be taken directly to Surgeon's Hall and there are several recorded instances of the 'dead' showing signs of life and being restored to consciouness. In most cases, sentence is deemed to have been carried out, or is commuted. In 1705, John Smith hangs at Tyburn for 15 minutes before a general cry of "Reprieve!" from the crowd results in him being cut down and taken to a nearby house, where he slowly recovers. Asked what it is like to be hanged, Smith has this to say:

When I was turned off, I was, for some time, sensible of very great pain occasioned by the weight of my body and felt my spirits in strange commotion, violently pressing upwards. Having forced their way to my head I saw a great blaze or glaring light that seemed to go out of my eyes in a flash and then I lost all sense of pain. After I was cut down, I began to come to myself and the blood and spirits forcing themselves into their former channels put me by a prickling or shooting into such intolerable pain that I could have wished those hanged who had cut me down.

Unmasking the Victorian hangman

For condemned murderers and rapists, highway robbers, 'utterers' of false coin and people like William Potter (convicted of cutting down an orchard) the last person to see them alive is the hangman. A succession of men occupy this singular position. Most are seemingly ordinary people: some are tradesmen such as cobblers and at least two families pass the secrets of the trade down from father to son.

These hangmen live extraordinary lives, some playing to the crowds at public executions and selling used rope at so much an inch and others travelling incognito to executions in distant prisons by train. One or two treat themselves with the respect they believe is due to a government official: James Berry prints his own business cards, 'James Berry, Executioner' appearing incongruously beneath a pretty sprig of foliage. In fact, the public's respect for the hangman often depends on his demeanour and proficiency, and drunken or inefficient hangmen at public executions can expect a rough reception.

The hangman's relationship with his victims is, of course, an unusual one. Before William Calcraft invents the strap which pinions prisoners' arms to their sides, the hands of the condemned are tied in front, so they can pray and, as sometimes happens, the hangman can shake hands with them before reaching for the lever. Some hangmen have already made the acquaintance of the people they hang. Before the hood is slipped over their heads, a few condemned felons may recognise the man who ties their hands and places the noose around their necks as a fellow criminal. This is because in the early part of the century, it is not unusual for the hangman to be a prisoner, someone whose life has been spared on condition that he hangs other criminals. Others are men who have volunteered for the job and you have to wonder about the motives of those whose idea of steady employment involves carrying out executions.

Before the employment of hangmen is regularised, it is only necessary to apply to the governor of the prison holding the condemned man. The office of executioner has been a salaried position but once piece rate is introduced and the number of capital crimes is slashed, the reasons for taking such employment are less than clear.

Not surprisingly, the job attracts some curious applicants. William Calcraft, who was born in Great Baddow, Essex in 1800, is the nineteenth century's longest-serving practitioner of this black art, though 'art', black or otherwise, is perhaps too elevated a term for what Calcraft practises. While selling pies on Newgate hanging days, Calcraft strikes up an acquaintance with the hangman, through whom he is able to inveigle himself within the walls of the prison. Initially employed to flog juvenile miscreants, he soon secures the office he will hold for 45 years and in which he will hang some 450 men and women.

Calcraft uses the 'short drop' method, meaning that those he hangs can sometimes take several minutes to die, unless he enters the pit below and swings on their legs. William Bousfield's execution (see Chapter Six) isn't the only one he bungles. Other hangmen try to bring a degree of professionalism to the calling. William Marwood, another cobbler, takes a scientific view. He believes that breaking the neck with a longer drop will result in more a humane death than the grisly spectacles provided by Calcraft. The long drop had been invented by doctors in Ireland, but Marwood develops it and successfully executes William Frederick Horry in 1872. His successor, James Berry refines the long drop with a set of mathematical tables which suggest the length of drop to be given to people of different weights in order to ensure that the neck is broken and unconsciousness, if not death itself, is instantaneous.

Not that Berry didn't suffer his setbacks. His drop all but decapitates one prisoner, while he famously fails to execute John 'Babbacombe' Lee at Exeter Prison in 1885. Lee, a thief convicted of the murder of his employer, is brought to the scaffold, then hooded and noosed. When the lever is pulled, the trapdoor fails to open. Lee is removed from the scaffold while the doors are tested and found to be working. The prisoner is brought back to the trap and the same thing happens. After this dreadful process has been repeated for a third time, a message is sent to the Home Secretary, William Harcourt, who commutes Lee's sentence to one of life imprisonment.

For the first few decades of the nineteenth century, little has changed. Executions are still carried out in public and still draw thousands of spectators. With the coming of the railways, they attract hordes of ghoulish day trippers, too. London's executions are now held outside Newgate prison, or on the roofs of other prisons, which is a great improvement in the view of the authorities charged with carrying them out. There is no longer the two-hour procession through sometimes charged crowds and they save the huge expense of the escort, too. For the prisoners themselves, it just means that they arrive at the drop a good deal sooner.

Executions, now generally carried out with the short drop method, still result in slow deaths and, as in the case of 29-year-old William Bousfield, who killed his wife and three children with a razor, are sometimes bungled. Richard Clark reports that "on the eve of his execution, he...attempted suicide by throwing himself on the fire in the condemned cell, sustaining facial burns...his face was bandaged up and he had to be carried to the scaffold the following morning". Clark says that as the drop fell, Bousfield somehow managed to "get back onto the side of the platform and had to be pushed down by one of the warders, because Calcraft had fled from the gallows as a threat had been made to kill him the previous day. He was called back to find that Bousfield had again got his feet back onto the platform and in the end, had to jump down and hang onto Bousfield's legs to complete the execution". It was, Clark comments, "hardly a dignified ending and not one that went down well with spectators".

It seems doubtful that public executions are effective deterrents.

The holiday mood of the eighteenth century crowds and the little more decorous behaviour of nineteenth century ones (the cry of "hats off" when the condemned mounts the platform has more to do with obstructed views than consideration for the prisoner about to die) suggests that though the effect of the spectacle is often profound, the experience is more akin to a grisly public entertainment than a salutory lesson in punitive justice. The execution of Elizabeth Martha Brown outside Dorchester Prison has a questionable effect on the 16-year-old, future novelist Thomas Hardy. Brown had killed her husband with an axe after he had taken a whip to her. 'What a fine figure she showed against the sky as she hung in the misty rain', he writes, 'and how the tight black silk gown set off her shape as she wheeled half-round and back'. It is a scene which will stay with him all his life and which he will draw on, three decades later, to conclude *Tess of the d'Urbervilles*.

The mechanics of a hanging at Newgate are described matter-of-factly to John Binny, by the prison's deputy governor:

> *The scaffold is erected immediately before an execution. The workmen commence about one o'clock in the morning and finish about six o'clock. Executions generally take place on the Monday morning. The wooden fences around the scaffold to keep back the spectators are generally put up on the Monday. The scaffold is about the size of a large caravan, the sides being let down and a beam erected over it. The floor is composed of two parts, constructed so as to fall down to each side. The executioner touches a handle similar to a common pump handle which detaches the bolt underneath, and the murderer is suspended by the neck in presence of the vast confluence of people. He generally hangs for one hour, when a coffin is brought and placed under the body. The executioner, in presence of the Sheriffs...takes hold of the body and puts it into the coffin, after having cut the rope. The coffin is then brought into one of the wards of the prison and is afterwards buried in the interior of Newgate in the afternoon of the same day.*

But slowly, public hanging is losing its appeal and though the crowds still appear, many find the spectacle distasteful at least and campaign for the ending of public execution. Among many influential personages watching the execution of 23-year-old Swiss valet Francois Courvoisier (convicted of murdering his master, Lord William Russell) is the novelist William Makepeace Thackeray, who afterwards calls the business a "hideous debauchery". Charles Dickens attends the execution of husband and wife murderers Frederick and Maria Manning, but seems more revolted by the behaviour of his fellow spectators. "The horrors of the gibbet and of the crime which brought the wretched murderers to it faded in my mind", he says, "before the atrocious bearing, looks, and language of the assembled spectators."

Dickens's view is representative of a new mood that is abroad, one which appears to associate the grisly spectacle of public executions with the unrefined boorishness of another age. Modern Victorian Britain has moved on and although as Clark notes, the 1864 Royal Commission on Capital Punishment 'concluded that there was no case for abolition of the death penalty' it does recommend the ending of public executions. The final public execution is that of Michael Barrett, a Fenian convicted of the murders of a number of people, who die when he explodes a bomb at the Clerkenwell House of Detention as he attempts to free another Fenian. William Calcraft executes 27-year-old Barrett in front of Newgate Prison.

Although future executions are held within prison walls, hanging at the end of a rope continues to be the ultimate punishment for those who have transgressed the law. Far fewer crimes, though, are punishable by death. The 1830s sees many crimes removed from the long list of capital ones. By the end of the decade, you can no longer be executed for stealing a sheep or cutting down an orchard, and nor do coiners and forgers, sodomists and rapists find themselves toeing the trap. Much of this is the work of Sir Robert Peel, whose reforms have as much to do with tidying up and making sense of a messy accumulation of statutes (leading to one man being hanged for a crime while another is not), as an act of humanity. It isn't until John Russell becomes Home Secretary in 1835 that the number of death sentences carried out shows significant signs of decrease.

However, by 1861, the days of prisoners being condemned together in batches are history and the death sentence itself is now applicable only in cases of murder, piracy, arson in a royal dockyard, espionage and high treason.

Glossary of Criminal Slang

Area sneak	thief accessing house by lower yard
Barking iron	pistol
Beak	magistrate
Beak hunting	stealing poultry
Beef	hue-and-cry
Bellows	lungs
Benculls	friends
Betty	lock pick
Bill	handkerchief
Bit faker	counterfeiter
Blow	inform
Blow up	scold
Bludger	violent thug
Blue bottle	policeman
Bluey hunter	steals lead from house roofs
Boozing-ken	public house
Broadsman	card sharp
Bug hunters	robbers of drunks
Bull	five shillings
Buzzing	thieving
Cannister	head
Cant	thieves' talk
Chavy	child
Chirped	informed
Chiv	blade (weapon)
Choker	neckcloth
Clever nob in the fur trade	barrister
Cly	waistcoat pocket
Coiner	counterfeiter of coins
Cove	man
Cracksman	burglar
Crib	lodging or building

Crow	one looking out while crime is committed
Crusher	policeman
Davy's dust	gunpowder
Dead lurkers	steal coats and umbrellas in dark passages
Dipper	pickpocket
Dollymop	amateur prostitute
Drag sneaks	steal luggage and goods from carts and coaches
Drumsticks	legs
Drummers	render victims insensible by use of drugs
Dumpling depot	stomach
Dunsman	turnkey or jailor
Fakement	forgery
Fan, to	to feel pockets prior to 'dipping'
Fart catcher	footman (who walks behind master or mistress)
Fences	receivers of stolen goods
Fizzing	(superlative) good
Floating Academy, the	hulk, or prison ship
Fogle	silk handkerchief
Gropus	pocket
Ivories	teeth
Jemmy	burglar's tool
Judy	woman or prostitute
Jug	prison
Kingsman	type of handkerchief
Lagged	transported
Light-fingered gentry	pickpockets
London Particular	'pea soup' fog
Lush	alcohol
Lushing ken	drinking establishment
Magsman	skittle sharper or minor conman
Maltooler	thief preying on omnibus passengers

GLOSSARY OF CRIMINAL SLANG

Mawleys	hands
Mobsmen	pickpockets
Mudlarks	scavengers of items from riverbanks or berthed ships
Needful, the	money
Noisy racket men	steal glass and china
Nosed	informed
Padding-ken	low lodging house
Pannie	burglary
Parish prig	chaplain
Penny gaff	low theatre
Prima donnas	superior prostitutes
Prop nailers	steal pins and brooches
Queer screens	forged notes
Ray	one shilling and sixpence
Resurrectionists	steal dead bodies
Sawney hunters	steal bacon from cheesemongers' doorways
Skinners	women who steal the clothes of children
Smashers	pass counterfeit money into circulation
Smatter hauling	stealing handkerchiefs
Sneaksmen	stealthy sneak thieves
Snoozer	robs passengers staying at railway hotels
Snow gatherers	steal washing from hedges
Star glazing	cutting holes in shop windows to steal goods
Stock buzzers	stealers of handkerchiefs
Stunner	something considered very good
Swell	well dressed man
Tail buzzers	those who steal from coat pockets
Tile	hat
Till frisker	one who robs from the till in the shopman's absence

Tin	money
Toshers	hunt coppers and small valuables along the river shore
Tuck-up fair	gallows
Up the spout	to pawn something
Wires	pickpockets who target ladies

Bibliography

Arnold, Catherine, *City of Sin London and its Vices* (Simon & Schuster, 2010)

Balfour, J.S., *My Prison Life* (Chapman and Hall, 1907)

Binny, John; Hemyng, Bracebridge; Mayhew, Henry, *The Criminal Prisons of London* (Griffin, Bohn, and Company 1862)

Campbell, Charles, *The Intolerable Hulks, British Shipboard Confinement 1776 – 1857* (Heritage Books, 1994)

Clark, Richard, *Capital Punishment in Britain*, (Ian Allen, 2009)

Davies, Andrew, *The Map of London From 1746 to the Present Day* (BT Batsford LTD, 1987)

Dickens, Charles, *Oliver Twist* (1838)
— *Sketches by Boz* (1833-1836)

Douglas, David C., *English Historical Documents XII 1833-1872* (Eyre & Spottiswode, 1956)

Fielding, Steve, *The Hangman's Record Volume One 1868-1899* (Chancery House Press, 1994)

Fitzgerald, Michael, *Ragged London* (The History Press, 2011)

Gaunt, Richard A., *Sir Robert Peel* (IB Tauris, 2010)

Handcock, G. M.; Young, W. G. *English Historical Documents 1833-1874* (Eyre & Spottiswoode, 1964)

Hawkings, David, *Criminal Ancestors A Guide to Historical Criminal Records in England and Wales* (Alan Sutton, 1992)

Mayhew, Henry, *London Labour & The London Poor* (Dover, 1968)
— *London's Underworld* (Spring Books, 1950)

Picard, Liza, *Victorian London* (Wiedenfield, 2005)

Porter, Roy, *London A Social History* (Hamish Hamilton, 1994)

Priestly, Philip, *Victorian Prison Lives* (Pimlico, 1985)

de Quincey, Thomas, *Miscellaneous Essays*

Read, Donald, *Peel and the Victorians* (Blackwell, 1987)

Thomas, Donald, *The Victorian Underworld* (John Murray, 1998)

White, Jerry, *London In The Nineteenth Century: 'A Human Awful Wonder of God'* (Vintage Digital, 2011)

Websites

The Art of Manliness: *artofmanliness.com*

British Women's Emancipation Since the Renaissance: *historyofwomen.org*

Casebook: Jack the Ripper: *casebook.org*

Dickens and London.com: *dickens-and-london.com*

Gendocs: Victorian London Research: *homepage.ntlworld.com/hitch/gendocs/police*

The Great Wen – A London Blog: *greatwen.com*

History Today magazine: *historytoday.com*

London and Literature in the Nineteenth Century: *cf.ac.uk/encap/skilton/fullidx.html*

Mostly Victorian: *mostly-victorian.com*

Out of this Century: *outofthiscentury.wordpress.com*

Victorian London: *victorianlondon.org*

Victorian Slang Glossary: *tlucretius.net/Sophie/Castle/victorian_slang*

Writing Women's History: *writingwomenshistory.blogspot.co.uk*

Index

INDEX

Uncover the stories of black sheep ancestors – at *findmypast.co.uk*

Tracing your family tree can lead to many surprises, not least locating a relative with a colourful past – whether they were convicted felons or victims of a crime. Many of these people lived on the margins of society and uncovering more information about them can seem like a difficult process. However, you'll find it much easier if you make full use of all available public records, and the best way to do so is to search them online.

At *www.findmypast.co.uk* you'll find millions of digitised records to help you discover your heritage or flesh out the stories behind your family tree. In addition to the census, parish registers, occupational records and institution registers, Britain's leading family history website has a huge range of records on crime, prisons and punishments. Simple to search and with original documents available on screen in seconds, it is both the ideal starting point for researchers and a brilliant resource to help more experienced genealogists uncover new information.

• Follow an individual through the records from their misdemeanour to the sentence they received. After their release, find out whether they decided to go straight or returned to a life of crime.

• Come face-to-face with your forebear through the original police photographs and physical descriptions of criminals preserved on thousands of records.

• The British authorities transported men, women and children across the world for as little as stealing a watch or a couple of coins. Search the departure lists to find those shipped to Australia.

• Due to overcrowding, thousands of prisoners were kept on former warships, known as hulks, often in terrible conditions. Was your unlucky ancestor among them?

• Children, as well as adults were once imprisoned for petty crimes. You may discover that your family member embarked on a life of crime at a tender age!

Read all about them!

If your ancestor hit the headlines due to their involvement in a criminal case, then you can easily access scans of original news reports through a simple online search. Findmypast.co.uk is working with the British Library to digitise its collection of local British newspapers and already has over 6.5 million pages from 1710 to 1963 online. You can search these by using the names of ancestors, dates, locations and key words. Search the newspapers at: *www.findmypast.co.uk/search/newspapers*

**Find out more about available records
and pricing at
*www.findmypast.co.uk***